Student Study Guide

To Accompany

Second Edition

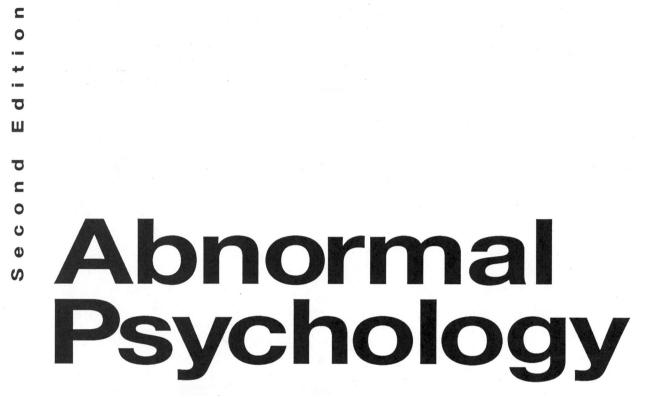

Abnormal Psychology

The Human Experience of Psychological Disorders

Richard P. Halgin
University of Massachusetts at Amherst

Susan Krauss Whitbourne
University of Massachusetts at Amherst

Brown & Benchmark
PUBLISHERS

Madison, WI   Dubuque   Guilford, CT   Chicago   Toronto   London
Mexico City   Caracas   Buenos Aires   Madrid   Bogotá   Sydney

ISBN 0-697-27559-0

Printed in the United States of America by Times Mirror Higher Education Group, Inc., 2460 Kerper Boulevard, Dubuque, Iowa, 52001

10 9 8 7 6 5 4 3 2 1

CONTENTS

Preface   i

1   Understanding Abnormality: A Look at History and Research   1

2   Classification, Treatment Plans, Ethics, and Legal Issues   9

3   Assessment   19

4   Psychodynamic and Humanistic Perspectives   28

5   Family Systems, Behavioral, and Biological Perspectives   38

6   Personality Disorders   46

7   Anxiety Disorders   56

8   Somatoform Disorders, Psychophysiological Conditions, and Dissociative Disorders   65

9   Sexual Disorders   75

10   Mood Disorders   85

11   Schizophrenia and Related Disorders   93

12   Development-Related Disorders   106

13   Cognitive Disorders   115

14   Substance-Related Disorders   127

15   Impulse-Control Disorders and Eating Disorders   137

Preface

This Study Guide is designed to serve as a valuable accompaniment to *Abnormal Psychology: The Human Experience of Psychological Disorders, Second Edition* by Richard P. Halgin and Susan Krauss Whitbourne. By paging through the textbook, you will notice that there is so much to learn -- concepts and terms, historically important facts, and complex theories. Most students find it helpful to have assistance in organizing the material and making their study time most efficient. You will find that this Study Guide helps you achieve these goals, and adds an exciting twist by making the information fun to learn. Here are a few of the features of this Study Guide that you will find particularly valuable:

Clear and Innovative Study Elements

In addition to traditional elements such as multiple choice items and matching tests, you will find innovative aids to learning and studying the material in the textbook. Of particular note are the engaging and creative games and puzzles designed by one of the textbook authors, Susan Krauss Whitbourne. The Study Guide for the First Edition was used by thousands of students, whose evaluations were filled with enthusiastic comments about how much they enjoyed studying the material because of the "brain-teasing" techniques.

Answers to Textbook Thought Questions

Throughout the textbook you will find dozens of brief clinical cases, each of which is accompanied by two thought questions. Answers to these thought questions are provided in the Study Guide. By first trying to answer the questions yourself, and then comparing your answers to those in the Study Guide, you will be able to assess your level of understanding of the issues raised in the textbook.

Glossary Study Cards

To assist you in your learning the hundreds of terms associated with abnormal psychology, the Study Guide includes Glossary Study Cards. These cards, which have a glossary term on one side and the term's definition on the other side, are fun and easy-to-use study aids. You can sort them any number of ways. For example, you can select those pertaining to the chapters on which you are about to be tested. Or, you can sort the cards according to your level of understanding of the terms, moving a card from the "least understood" to the "somewhat understood" to the "most understood" pile as you proceed through the process of correctly defining and understanding each term.

Using these elements, here is what we recommend to be an effective sequence for learning the material:

1.   Prior to reading the textbook chapter, review the questions in the Study Guide. Make notes about the material that seems particularly challenging or unfamiliar to you, so that when you read the textbook chapter you will be looking for that material.

2.   Read the textbook chapter and take notes in the way that you customarily find to be most effective.

3.   After reading the textbook chapter, turn to the Study Guide and complete the exercises, in order to determine how well you understand what you have just studied.

4.   Score your answers and determine the areas that require more intensive study. Then return to the textbook, paying particular attention to the information that was previously difficult for you.

In this Study Guide, we have attempted to encourage you to take an active role in mastering the material by using multiple approaches to learning the major concepts and ideas covered in the textbook. We hope that you find these exercises to be engaging, challenging, and useful.

CHAPTER 1
UNDERSTANDING ABNORMALITY:
A LOOK AT HISTORY AND RESEARCH

LEARNING OBJECTIVES

1.0 What is Abnormal Behavior?
    1.1 Recognize that it is difficult to define abnormal behavior because it overlaps with "normal" behavior.
    1.2 Contrast the view of abnormal behavior as deviation from the average with the view of abnormal behavior as deviation from the optimal.
    1.3 Define abnormal behavior as a concept that incorporates biological, psychological, and sociocultural dimensions.
2.0 Abnormal Psychology Throughout History
    2.1 Recognize the influence of beliefs about possession on prehistoric approaches to psychological disorders.
    2.2 Indicate how the beliefs of Hippocrates and Galen contributed to a scientific approach to understanding abnormal behavior.
    2.3 Explain the return in the Middle Ages to the belief that abnormal behavior is caused by demonic or spiritual possession, and how this belief was reflected in the treatment of the mentally ill.
    2.4 Describe the reform movement in Europe and the U.S. in the 1700s and the contributions of Chiarugi, Pinel, Tuke, Rush, and Dix.
    2.5 Explain the contributions of psychiatrists such as Greisinger and Kraepelin to contemporary medical approaches to treating the mentally ill.
    2.6 Describe the influence of Freudian psychoanalysis on the treatment of psychological disorders and the impact of its predecessors such as Braid, Mesmer, Liébault, Bernheim, and Charcot.
    2.7 Indicate how somatic treatments such as psychosurgery and electroconvulsive therapy were used and abused as treatment methods for people in institutions.
    2.8 Explain the pros and cons of the deinstitutionalization movement and the components of successful community treatment programs.
3.0 Research Methods in Abnormal Psychology
    3.1 Describe the essential elements of the scientific method, including observation, hypothesis formation, and sampling.
    3.2 Explain the experimental method, and describe the concepts of independent and dependent variables, placebos, treatment and control groups, double-blind technique, the quasi-experimental design, and demand characteristics.
    3.3 Discuss the correlational method and define negative and positive correlations.
    3.4 Outline the survey method and distinguish prevalence from incidence.
    3.5 Describe the case-study method.
    3.6 Indicate how the single-subject study is conducted, and how the multiple baseline technique is used in this type of research.
    3.7 Explain the logic and procedures involved in studies of genetic influence, including twin studies, adoption studies, crossfostering studies, biological marker studies, and genetic mapping research.
4.0 The Human Experience of Psychological Disorders
    4.1 Describe the impact of psychological disorder on the individual's life.
    4.2 Explain the concept of stigma as it applies to an individual with a psychological disorder.
    4.3 List the myths regarding psychological disorders and explain why they are myths.
    4.4 Indicate how psychological disorders affect the family, community, and society.

5.0 Chapter Boxes

    5.1 Describe the importance of the study in which psychologists disguised themselves as psychiatric patients and sought admission to a hospital.

    5.2 Discuss cultural variations in defining what is "abnormal" behavior.

    5.3 Indicate the relationship between creativity and mental illness as described in research on writers and artists.

IDENTIFYING HISTORICAL PERIODS

Put the letter corresponding to the historical period in the blank next to each approach to psychological disorder:

P= Prehistoric   **S**= 1700s

A= Ancient Greece and Rome   **E**= 1800s to 1900s (approximately to 1950)

M= Middle Ages and Renaissance   **T**= Late 20th century (1950 and later)

Period	**Approach to Psychological Disorders**
1. _____	Reliance on superstition, alchemy, and astrology as explanations of psychological disorders.
2. _____	Emphasis on dysfunction of the brain as the cause of psychological disorder.
3. _____	First documented recognition of the role of emotional disturbances in causing psychological disorders.
4. _____	Use of mesmerism to redistribute disturbed bodily fluids thought to cause psychological disorder.
5. _____	First reform efforts made to remove patients from chains and other physical restraints.
6. _____	Punishment and execution of people thought to be witches.
7. _____	Development of managed care as an approach to outpatient treatment.
8. _____	Widespread use of electroconvulsive therapy and psychosurgery for treating psychological disorder.
9. _____	Large-scale release of patients from psychiatric hospitals into treatment sites in the community.
10. _____	Transformed poorhouses into asylums where psychologically disturbed individuals were punished.
11. _____	Rise of the medical model as an explanation of psychological disorder.
12. _____	Development of moral treatment as an approach to care for people with psychological disorder.
13. _____	Holes drilled in heads of people with psychological disorders as a method of releasing evil spirits.
14. _____	Growth of large publicly funded institutions designed for people with psychological disorders.

"CATTERGORIES"

This puzzle is based on a popular board game in which contestants must think of an item in a specified category that begins with a certain letter. Each of the groups below contains items with the same first letter. Provide the answer in the space provided.

P

_____ French hospital staff worker in the 1700s who influenced Pinel to free patients from their chains.

_____ Belief based in spirituality that the cause of psychological disorders lies in demonic control.

_____ Model of treatment for psychological disorders based on the notion of unconscious determinants.

_____ Control condition in an experiment in which subjects believe they are receiving treatment.

_____ Entire group of people sharing a characteristic of interest to a researcher, from which a sample is derived.

S

_____ Negative label that is applied to people with psychological disorders.

_____ Approach to investigation that involves observations, hypothesis testing, and controls.

_____ Englishman living in the 1500s who challenged the belief that demonic possession caused psychological disorder.

_____ 20th century American psychiatrist who claims that mental illness is a "myth."

_____ Explanation of psychological disorders that focuses on violation of norms and potential harm to others.

H

_____ Greek philosopher who proposed that imbalance of bodily fluids produced psychological disorder.

_____ Term coined by the English physician Braid to describe process of putting a person into a trance.

_____ Disorder treated by Freud and Breuer in which psychological problems are expressed in physical form.

_____ Prediction of a certain outcome in an experiment.

_____ Greek philosopher who believed that rationality depended on the nature of fire within the soul.

MATCHING

Put the letter from the right-hand column corresponding to the correct match in the blank next to each item in the left-hand column.

1. ___ Research method in which the association is observed between two variables.

2. ___ The group in an experiment that does not receive the treatment being tested.

3. ___ Researcher who conducted a study in which "pseudopatients" were admitted to psychiatric hospitals.

4. ___ In an experiment, the variable whose value is observed after the manipulation is performed.

5. ___ Research method in which each person is studied in both the experimental and control conditions.

6. ___ Physician who, in the mid-1500s, criticized the prevailing views of psychological disorder as caused by demonic possession.

7. ___ American living in the 1800s who was an influential reformer of treatment of psychologically disturbed people.

8. ___ British psychiatrist who proposed that people who follow society's norms are more disturbed than those who refuse to do so.

9. ___ In an experiment, the variable whose value is set by the researcher.

10. ___ Treatment method discovered by Freud and Breuer in the case of Anna O. in which the client talks about emotional conflicts.

11. ___ Roman physician who studied psychological disorder through experimental, scientific methods.

12. ___ General name for the type of research method in which the investigator attempts to establish cause-effect relations.

13. ___ The group in an experiment that receives the treatment being tested.

14. ___ Type of study on genetic influences in which children of normal parents are adopted by parents with psychological disorders.

15. ___ Experimental approach in which neither the researcher nor the subject is aware of which condition the subject is in.

a. experimental method
b. Laing
c. double-blind
d. dependent variable
e. Weyer
f. cathartic
g. experimental group
h. Rosenhan
i. Dix
j. correlational
k. Galen
l. cross-fostering study
m. independent variable
n. single subject design
o. control group

SHORT ANSWER

1. Place an "X" next to the word or name that does not belong:

a. R.D. Laing
   Thomas Szasz
   William Greisinger
   David Rosenhan

b. Dorothea Dix
   Vincenzo Chiarugi
   Phillipe Pinel
   James Braid

c. multiple baselines
   representativeness
   demand characteristics
   mesmerism

d. pragmatic
   sanguine
   choleric
   phlegmatic

e. Jean-Martin Charcot
   Benjamin Rush
   Josef Breuer
   Ambrose-Auguste Liébault

2. Match the period of history with the predominant orientation or orientations to understanding and treating psychological disorders by filling in the blank with the letter representing the predominant orientation. Historical periods associated with more than one orientation have two blanks:

Period of history

__   Prehistorical times
__   Ancient Greece and Rome
__ __   Middle Ages and Renaissance
__   Europe and the U.S. in the 1700s
__   1800s to 1900s
__ __   Late 20th century

Predominant orientation(s)

S= Scientific
H= Humanitarian
M= Mystical

3. Answer the following questions concerning the Research Focus entitled "How 'Crazy' are Creative People?" :

a. What research method was used by Andreasen?

_____

_____

b. Why was it necessary to include a group of people who were comparable in age, sex, and education to the writers?

_____

_____

c. Why would it have been preferable for Andreasen to have conducted the study without knowing which subjects were creative writers and which were controls?

_____

_____

4. Using the criteria outlined in the text for defining abnormality as deviation from the "average" (A) vs. deviation from the "optimal" (O), evaluate each of the following behaviors in terms of which of these criteria it meets:

Behavior	Type of deviation
a. A woman receives an unusually high score on a test of depression.	_____
b. A man laughs at the sad part of a movie.	_____
c. A college student makes a mistake when giving a well-prepared oral presentation due to feelings of tension.	_____
d. An athlete is unrealistically self-critical for a team's failure to win a game.	_____
e. A boy is highly active compared to his classmates.	_____
f. A teenager refuses to join her friends for a party because of her extreme shyness.	_____
g. A man with a long record of arrests feels no remorse after robbing a convenience store.	_____
h. A woman is unable to stop herself from pulling out her own hair.	_____
i. A sports fan knows the statistics on all members of nationally known hockey teams.	_____

5. For each of the criteria for deviant behavior, describe the nature of the criterion, its applicability, and its limitations.

Criterion	Definition	Applicability	Limitations
Biological			
Psychological			
Sociocultural			

6. a. Describe four ways in which families are affected by the presence of a psychologically disturbed member:

_____

_____

_____

b. What has been an organized response of groups of families to these difficulties?

_____

c. How are local communities affected by the presence of people with psychological disorder?

_____

7. a. What is the significance of the fact that a disorder has a higher concordance rate among monozygotic compared to dizygotic twins?

_____

b. Describe the major difference between an adoption study and a cross-fostering study:

_____

c. What is the purpose of studies on biological markers?

_____

MULTIPLE CHOICE

1. Jackson is elated because his exam grade was substantially higher than the mean of the class. Jackson's exam grade would be considered a deviation from:
   a. the average.
   b. the optimal.
   c. the mode.
   d. the ideal.

2. Which American psychiatrist has argued that the concept of mental illness is a "myth" created in modern society and put into practice by the mental health profession?
   a. R. D. Laing
   b. David Rosenhan
   c. Thomas Szasz
   d. Marie Balter

3. Trephining is the term used for the procedure in which:
   a. holes were drilled in a disturbed person's skull in order to release evil spirits.
   b. a ritual involving fire was used to invoke healthy mental energy as a replacement for unhealthy energy.
   c. blood was released from a person in the belief that an overabundance of blood caused unpredictable mood shifts.
   d. an individual was restrained in a "tranquilizer" chair.

4. Which theorist proposed that bodily fluids -- black bile, yellow bile, phlegm, and blood -- influence physical and mental health?
   a. Hippocrates
   b. Galen
   c. Eysenck
   d. Pinel

5. Which research method would most likely be used by a researcher interested in determining the relationship between IQ and level of anxiety?
   a. experimental
   b. case study
   c. single-subject design
   d. correlational

6. In 1792, an English Quaker named William Tuke established the York Retreat. Succeeding generations of Tuke's family carried on his work by using methods known as:
   a. the "well-cure".
   b. the medical model.
   c. moral treatment.
   d. spiritual treatment.

7. The American Psychiatric Association was greatly influenced by Greisinger's 1845 book on the pathology and treatment of psychological disorders that focused on the role in abnormal behavior of:
   a. hormonal imbalances.
   b. demonic influence.
   c. early life experience.
   d. brain dysfunction.

8. Anton Mesmer claimed that psychological cures could be brought about:
   a. through the use of hypnosis.
   b. by redistributing the magnetic fluids in a person's body.
   c. through use of the cathartic method.
   d. by using psychoanalytic techniques.

9. The deinstitutionalization movement involved:
   a. the restructuring of psychiatric institutions to make them more humane.
   b. the large-scale release of psychiatric clients into the community.
   c. the movement of psychiatric patients from public institutions to private institutions.
   d. the recognition that mental illness is a "myth."

10. A researcher makes sure that her sample of voters accurately reflects the population of all voters in a given election so that it meets the criterion of:
    a. representativeness.
    b. randomness.
    c. control.
    d. probability.

11. A Chinese man who "speaks" to his dead relatives is an example of which aspect of abnormal behavior?
    a. attempting to "fake" schizophrenia
    b. genetic mapping
    c. the influence of religious beliefs
    d. mesmerism

12. A researcher tests the effectiveness of a medication so that neither the person administering nor the person receiving the treatment knows whether the subject is in the control or the experimental group. What is this technique?
    a. demand characteristic
    b. correlational
    c. experimental
    d. double-blind

13. Which of the following is considered to be a sociocultural criterion for defining abnormality?
    a. personal distress
    b. maladaptive behavior
    c. statistical deviation
    d. violated social conventions

14. A label that causes certain people to be regarded as different is referred to as a:
    a. role.
    b. norm.
    c. stigma.
    d. diagnosis.

15. Which of the following is a potential reason why some people often joke about mental illness?
    a. Deep down, all people are psychologically repressed.
    b. People often joke about issues that make them anxious.
    c. Most people have the potential to become mentally ill.
    d. People are basically cruel and enjoy the suffering of others.

16. When did the scientific model of psychological disorders emerge?
    a. In prehistoric times.
    b. In ancient Greece and Rome.
    c. In the Middle Ages.
    d. In the 20th century.

17. Who is known as the founder of American psychiatry?
    a. Dorothea Dix
    b. Benjamin Rush
    c. William Tuke
    d. Clifford Beers

18. What was the most significant reason for the declining conditions in mental institutions during the later part of the reform period?
    a. overcrowding
    b. lack of funding
    c. undereducated staff
    d. reemergence of spiritual explanations

19. Who was primarily responsible for reform in American mental institutions?
    a. Benjamin Rush
    b. Clifford Beers
    c. Dorothea Dix
    d. William Godding

20. Which of the following methods is most effective for determining cause and effect relationships?
    a. The case study method.
    b. The correlational method.
    c. The survey method.
    d. The experimental method.

ANSWERS
IDENTIFYING HISTORICAL PERIODS

1. M	6. M	11. E
2. E	7. T	12. S
3. A	8. T	13. P
4. E	9. T	14. E
5. S	10. M	

CATTERGORIES

P	S	H
Pussin	Stigma	Hippocrates
Possession	Scientific	Hypnosis
Psychoanalysis	Scot	Hysteria
Placebo	Szasz	Hypothesis
Population	Sociocultural	Heraclitus

MATCHING

1. j		9. m	
2. o		10. f	
3. h		11. k	
4. d		12. a	
5. n		13. g	
6. e		14. l	
7. i		15. c	
8. b			

SHORT ANSWER

1.
   a. William Greisinger — Contemporary critics of medical model
   b. James Braid — 18th century reformers of treatment
   c. mesmerism — terms related to research methods
   d. pragmatic — the dispositions proposed by Hippocrates
   e. Benjamin Rush — physicians who developed hypnosis

2. M
   S
   M & H
   H
   S
   S & H

3. a. Correlational, because she was investigating the relationship between two naturally occurring phenomena.
    b. A control group of people with comparable age, sex, and education was needed to rule out the possibility that any observed relationship between creativity and psychological disorder was due to factors other than the backgrounds of the writers. This was an important aspect of the study, because as it turned out, there was a higher rate of psychological disorder in the "controls" than would be expected on statistical grounds.
    c. Because Andreasen knew the identity of her subjects, it might have been difficult for her to evaluate her hypothesis objectively. However, the fact that Andreasen found a relationship between creativity and mood disorder, not schizophrenia as she had predicted, suggests that her awareness of the subjects' identity did not bias her evaluation of their psychological status.
4. a. average; b. average; c. optimal; d. optimal; e. average; f. optimal; g. optimal; h. optimal; i. average

5.

Criterion	Definition	Applicability	Limitation
Biological	Disorder or dysfunction in a part of the body or aspect of biological functioning.	Biological factors play important role in cause, expression, and treatment of abnormal behavior.	Not relevant to all disorders.
Psychological	Disorder of emotional state, intellect, memory, language use, adaptation, ability to satisfy personal needs; feelings of personal distress.	Feelings of unhappiness and maladjustment are useful indicators of dysfunction.	People may show maladaptive behavior but not necessarily feel distressed.
Sociocultural	Violation of social norms.	Situations in which people behave unacceptably or cause harm to others.	Not every member of a society agrees regarding what is "acceptable."

6. a. Feeling the pain of the affected member.
        Worrying that the affected member will be harmed.
        Experiencing the stigma of the affected family member.
        Feeling blamed by the mental health profession for the person's problems.
    b. Families have formed support and education groups such as the National Alliance for the Mentally Ill. Books have also been written that specifically concern family issues.
    c. Halfway houses and day treatment centers may need to be established for deinstitutionalized individuals. In the absence of sufficient treatment programs, psychologically disturbed people may become part of the homeless population of a community.
7. a. The disorder probably has a genetic basis because monozygotic twins have identical genetic inheritance.
    b. In an adoption study, a child of biologically disordered parents is adopted by parents who have no psychological disorder; in a cross-fostering study, a child of normal parents is adopted by parents who have psychological disorders.
    c. In studies of biological markers, researchers attempt to understand the specific mechanisms involved in models of genetic transmission.

MULTIPLE CHOICE

1.	a	5.	d	9.	b	13.	d	17.	b
2.	c	6.	c	10.	a	14.	c	18.	a
3.	a	7.	d	11.	c	15.	b	19.	c
4.	a	8.	b	12.	d	16.	b	20.	d

CHAPTER 2
CLASSIFICATION, TREATMENT PLANS, ETHICS, AND LEGAL ISSUES

LEARNING OBJECTIVES

1.0 Psychological Disorder: Experiences of Client and Clinician
    1.1 Distinguish the concept of a "client" from that of a "patient" as the individual who is the focus of psychological treatment.
    1.2 Describe the types of clinicians who provide psychological treatment.

2.0 The Diagnostic and Statistical Manual of Mental Disorders
    2.1 Outline the history of the development of DSM-IV.
    2.2 Define the term "mental disorder" as it is used in DSM-IV.
    2.3 Explain the assumptions underlying the DSM-IV, including the medical model, atheoretical orientation, categorical approach, and multiaxial system.
    2.4 Define the five axes of DSM-IV:
        Axis I: Clinical Disorders
        Axis II: Personality Disorders and Mental Retardation
        Axis III: General Medical Conditions
        Axis IV: Psychosocial and Environmental Problems
        Axis V: Global Assessment of Functioning

3.0 The Diagnostic Process
    3.1 Explain how the clinician obtains the client's reported symptoms.
    3.2 Indicate how the diagnostic criteria of DSM-IV are used in identifying a possible diagnosis, including the role of the decision tree.
    3.3 Discuss the ways in which the clinician rules out differential diagnoses.
    3.4 Explain how the clinician arrives at a final diagnosis.
    3.5. Indicate how a case formulation is constructed.
    3.6 Describe the need for cultural formulations and how they are written.

4.0 Planning a Treatment
    4.1 Contrast short- and long-term goals of treatment.
    4.2 Distinguish the treatment sites of psychiatric hospitals, outpatient clinics, halfway houses and day treatment programs.
    4.3 Explain the various modalities of treatment, including individual psychotherapy, family therapy, group therapy, and milieu therapy.
    4.4 Discuss the role of the clinician's theoretical perspective as it influences the nature of treatment.

5.0 Implementing Treatment
    5.1 Indicate the roles of the clinician and client as they influence the course of treatment.
    5.2 Discuss the frustrations and possible limitations involved in providing effective psychological treatment.

6.0 Ethical and Legal Issues
    6.1 Define the concept of informed consent and discuss its relevance to psychological treatment.
    6.2 Explain the importance of confidentiality and the related concept of privileged communication, and discuss the exceptions to these principles such as duty to warn.
    6.3 Discuss the process of involuntary commitment as a means of protecting the client and others from the expression of dangerous behaviors.
    6.4 Indicate the importance of the client's right to treatment and various rights of clients such as a humane environment, liberty, and safety.
    6.5 Describe the client's right to refuse treatment and to live in the least restrictive alternative to an institution.

7.0 Forensic Issues in Psychological Treatment
  7.1 Describe the history of the insanity defense and the relevance of recent cases such as Jeffrey Dahmer, Lorena Bobbitt, and the Menendez brothers.
  7.2 Explain the concept of competency to stand trial.
8.0 Chapter Boxes
  8.1 Indicate how the right to refuse treatment has become a critical issue for homeless people with psychological disorders.
  8.2 Discuss the evidence regarding whether minority individuals are particularly vulnerable to psychological disorders.
  8.3 Evaluate research on the prediction of violent behavior.

MATCHING

Put the letter from the right-hand column corresponding to the correct match in the blank next to each item in the left-hand column.

1. ___ Consistency of measures or diagnoses.
2. ___ Responsibility of a clinician to warn a person of possible threat or danger presented by a client's behavior.
3. ___ Evaluation of a client's ability to participate in court proceedings on behalf of his or her own defense.
4. ___ Diagnostic dimension that applies to clinical syndromes.
5. ___ Illness seen in Latinos in which a frightening event causes the "soul" to leave the body, resulting in depression and somatic symptoms.
6. ___ Protection of information about a client obtained in the process of providing treatment.
7. ___ Structured community-based treatment program similar to that found in a psychiatric hospital.
8. ___ Common term that refers to behavior involving loss of contact with reality.
9. ___ Accuracy of a diagnosis or measure.
10. ___ Approach to treatment in a psychiatric hospital in which the total environment is structured to be therapeutic.
11. ___ Process through which a clinician systematically rules out alternative diagnoses.
12. ___ Axis in DSM for designating long-standing maladaptive features of personality.
13. ___ Explanation of a client's psychological status that accompanies a diagnosis.
14. ___ Primary disorder for which the client is seeking treatment.
15. ___ Disorder found in Malaysia in which a man experiences a violent outburst, usually following an insult.

a. validity
b. confidentiality
c. milieu therapy
d. differential diagnosis
e. Axis II of the DSM
f. susto
g. amok
h. case formulation
i. reliability
j. Axis I of the DSM
k. duty to warn
l. competency to stand trial
m. day treatment
n. principal diagnosis
o. psychosis

PSYCH-MAN CHALLENGE

Go around the page from start to finish, writing your answers in the blocks. As you check your answers, draw an "X" through the blocks for which your answers were correct, and see if you get to "FINISH" with all blocks crossed out.

Decision making process involving a series of logical steps	Therapy modality of sharing feelings with others.	Client's right to be informed about risks and benefits of treatment.	Multi-dimensional classification and diagnosis system.	The right to treatment with as little restraint as possible	The interface between psychology and the law	Scale on Axis V to assess overall functioning
Area of assessment unique to clinical psychologists						Treatment site for recently deinstitutionalized clients.
Term used to describe collection of related symptoms						Percentage of people in population with a certain disorder
Name of the manual used in making diagnoses	A person seeking psychological services	**START**		**FINISH**	Famous case from which insanity rule emerged.	Process of admitting person to treatment involuntarily

IDENTIFYING THE AXIS

Put the Roman numeral corresponding to the axis on the DSM represented by each of the symptoms or characteristics below:

I=   Clinical syndromes
II=   Personality disorders and mental retardation
III=   Physical disorders or conditions
IV=   Psychosocial and environmental problems
V=   Global assessment of functioning

Axis	Symptoms or characteristics	Axis	Symptoms or characteristics
1. ____	Brain damage that interferes with memory	7. ____	Recent unemployment
2. ____	Extreme sadness, guilt, and suicidality	8. ____	Gastric ulcer
3. ____	Mental retardation	9. ____	Symptom severity ratings
4. ____	Death of a spouse	10. ____	Severe anxiety in social situations
5. ____	Chronic bronchitis	11. ____	Deficient ability to carry out tasks of everyday living
6. ____	Personality characterized by constant dependency on others		

SHORT ANSWER

1. Match the legal case or ruling with the term reflecting the principle or legal process it served to establish:

Case	Principle or legal process
___ a. O'Connor v. Donaldson	1. need to "appreciate" wrongfulness of an act
___ b. Tarasoff v. Regents of the University of California	2. proof of "insanity" needed
	3. least restrictive alternative
___ c. M'Naghten	4. right to treatment
___ d. ALI	5. insanity defense
___ e. Durham Rule	6. product of "mental disease or defect"
___ f. Insanity Defense Reform Act	7. duty to warn
___ g. Wyatt v. Stickney	

2. Explain the three main assumptions of the DSM regarding mental disorders:

Assumption about mental disorder	Explanation
The disorder is clinically significant	
The disorder is reflected in a syndrome	
The disorder is associated with present distress, impairment, or risk	
The disorder is not a culturally sanctioned response	

3. For each step of the diagnostic process, describe elements that the clinician must consider:

Step in diagnostic process	Elements that clinician considers
Client's reported symptoms	
Diagnostic criteria	
Differential diagnosis	
Final diagnosis	
Case formulation	

4. For each of the following treatment sites, describe the type of services provided and the reasons for referring clients to each site:

Treatment site	Type of service provided	Reasons for referral
Psychiatric hospital		
Outpatient treatment		
Halfway house		
Day treatment		

5. Answer the following questions about the process of implementing treatment for psychological disorders:

a. What would lead a clinician to recommend family therapy rather than individual therapy?

_____
_____

b. How does family therapy differ from group therapy?

_____
_____

c. What is the role of a clinician's theoretical orientation in providing treatment?

_____
_____

d. How might the clinician's reactions to a client influence the course of treatment?

_____
_____

e. What is the client's role in the treatment process?

_____
_____

f. What are some of the obstacles that can interfere with successful outcomes of treatment?

_____
_____

6. Describe the aims of each successive edition of the DSM:

DSM Edition	Goal	Limitations
I		
II		
III		
III-R		
IV		

7. Answer each of the following questions about forensic issues in psychological treatment:

a. Why was there a difference in the outcome of the Jeffrey Dahmer case compared to the John Hinckley case?

_____

_____

b. What have been the major issues identified in legislation and judicial rulings regarding the definition of "insanity"?

_____

_____

c. What factors are assessed in determining a person's competency to stand trial?

_____

_____

d. How do clinicians attempt to balance the need to commit a person involuntarily to treatment against the individual's right to the least restrictive alternative?

_____

_____

e. What issues are involved in a clinician's protecting a client's confidentiality versus the need to notify potential victims of harm?

_____

_____

f. What are the basic components of treatment to which hospitalized clients are entitled by law?

_____

_____

MULTIPLE CHOICE

1. The defense used by Lorena Bobbitt, the woman who admitted that she cut off her husband's penis, was based on this principle:
   a. irresistible impulse
   b. imperfect self-defense
   c. right to refuse treatment
   d. guilty but mentally ill

2. A doctoral level clinician who has been trained as a medical doctor is called a:
   a. clinical psychologist.
   b. clinician.
   c. psychiatrist.
   d. neurophysiologist.

3. The DSM was developed to ensure that a given diagnosis would be consistently applied. This criterion is referred to as:
   a. reliability.
   b. validity.
   c. predictability.
   d. base rate.

4. What is the commonly used term for behavior involving a person's loss of contact with reality?
   a. neurosis
   b. psychosis
   c. derealization
   d. syndrome

5. Upon admission to a psychiatric hospital for bizarre behavior, Carlos states that he has diabetes. This medical information would be noted on ___ of DSM-IV:
   a. Axis I
   b. Axis II
   c. Axis III
   d. Axis IV

6. Matthew has recently been discharged from a psychiatric hospital and is moving to a facility with other discharged residents until ready to live independently. Such a facility is called a:
   a. day treatment center.
   b. community mental health center.
   c. milieu therapy center.
   d. halfway house.

7. Dr. Tobin explains to clients the risks and benefits of therapy as well as the nature and limits of confidentiality. These are standards of:
   a. informed consent.
   b. duty to warn.
   c. least restrictive alternative.
   d. competency to participate in treatment.

8. Tatiana Tarasoff's parents won their lawsuit because a staff psychologist had failed to adhere to which standard of practice?
   a. informed consent
   b. confidentiality
   c. commitment
   d. duty to warn

9. In epidemiological research on racial differences in rates of psychological disorders, reports of higher rates among Blacks appear due to:
   a. methodological problems.
   b. true racial differences.
   c. lack of recent data.
   d. prejudice by the researchers.

10. In a study conducted by Norwegian researchers on the prediction of violent behavior, it was concluded that the single best predictor is:
    a. gender.
    b. history of drug abuse.
    c. growing up in a violent subculture.
    d. a history of previous violence.

11. In the landmark case of Wyatt v. Stickney, Wyatt's suit was based on the state's failure to:
    a. warn patients of the dangers involved in institutionalization.
    b. provide adequate and humane treatment.
    c. screen out violent individuals.
    d. acquire informed consent from patients.

12. What is the term that refers to a client's likelihood of recovering from a disorder?
    a. prediction
    b. syndrome
    c. prognosis
    d. base rate

13. A collection of symptoms that together form a definable pattern is a:
    a. diagnosis.
    b. syndrome.
    c. prognosis.
    d. disorder.

14. Which model does the DSM adhere to?
    a. psychoanalytic
    b. behavioral
    c. mystical
    d. medical

15. Axis II of the DSM is used for:
    a. clinical syndromes.
    b. personality disorders and mental retardation.
    c. organic brain disorders.
    d. substance abuse disorders.

16. The process of ruling out possible alternative diagnoses is called:
    a. differential diagnosis.
    b. compound diagnosis.
    c. assessment of functioning.
    d. multiaxial diagnosis.

17. An analysis of the client's development and the factors that may have influenced the client's current emotional state is called a:
    a. diagnosis.
    b. prognosis.
    c. classification.
    d. case formulation.

18. What treatment site is usually recommended by a clinician when the client presents a risk of harming self or others?
    a. community mental health center
    b. psychiatric hospital
    c. halfway house
    d. outpatient treatment center

19. The case of Joyce Brown, a homeless woman from New York City, illustrated which aspect of client's rights?
    a. right to refuse treatment
    b. parens patriae
    c. right to privacy
    d. right to receive treatment

20. A determination of whether or not an individual is psychologically capable of testifying on his or her behalf in a court of law refers to:
    a. a part of the ALI guidelines.
    b. the Durham rule.
    c. guilt by reason of insanity.
    d. competency to stand trial.

ANSWERS

MATCHING

1.	i	4.	j	7.	m	10.	c	13.	h
2.	k	5.	f	8.	o	11.	d	14.	n
3.	l	6.	b	9.	a	12.	e	15.	g

PSYCH-MAN CHALLENGE

Decision tree	Group therapy	Informed consent	Multiaxial	Least restrictive alternative	Forensic psychology	GAS
Psycho-logical testing						Halfway house
Syndrome						Base rate
Diagnostic and Statistical Manual (DSM)	Client	**START**		**FINISH**	M'Naghten	Commitment

IDENTIFYING THE AXIS

1.	I	5.	III	8.	III
2.	I	6.	II	9.	V
3.	II	7.	IV	10.	I
4.	IV				

SHORT ANSWER

1.
a.	3	e.	6
b.	7	f.	2
c.	5	g.	4
d.	1		

2.

Assumption about "mental disorder"	Explanation
The disorder is clinically significant	Symptoms must be present to a significant degree and for a significant period of time.
The disorder is reflected in a syndrome	Individual symptoms or problematic behaviors are not sufficient for diagnosis as a mental disorder.
The disorder is associated with present distress, impairment, or risk	The behaviors or symptoms must involve some type of personal or social cost.
The disorder is not culturally sanctioned	The disorder is not expectable for one's society or culture.

3.

Step in diagnostic process	Elements that clinician considers
Client's reported symptoms	Comparing the client's statement of problems with diagnostic terms and concepts.
Diagnostic criteria	Clarify the nature of the client's symptoms and attempt to match them with diagnostic criteria by following the decision tree.
Differential diagnosis	Rule out alternative diagnoses.
Final diagnosis	Provide diagnoses and ratings on the five axes of the DSM.
Case formulation	Place into perspective the client's diagnosis in the context of the client's life history.

4.

Treatment site	Type of service provided	Reasons for referral
Psychiatric hospital	24-hour inpatient treatment which may include medical and psychotherapeutic interventions best offered in a setting with close monitoring and supervision.	Client at risk of harming self or others.
Outpatient treatment	Psychotherapy and counseling	Treatment site most frequently recommended unless hospitalization is needed.
Halfway house	Interaction with other deinstitutionalized clients and supervision by professional staff who can help clients develop skills needed for independent living.	Client is recently deinstitutionalized and is not yet ready for independent living.
Day treatment	Milieu treatment similar to that provided in a psychiatric hospital.	Client does not need to be hospitalized but needs structured support during the day.

5. a. The clinician determines that although one person is the "patient," this person's difficulties reflect problems in the family as a whole.
   b. In group therapy, participants are unrelated clients who work together to share their difficulties and problems in a setting where they can receive feedback, develop trust, and improve their interpersonal skills. In family therapy, the therapist works with related individuals as a system to help alleviate the distress of one individual member.
   c. Clinicians are often trained with particular theoretical orientations that form the basis for the services they provide. However, most clinicians adapt their own perspective and combine it with elements of other perspectives to tailor their treatment to the needs of the individual client.
   d. Each client stimulates a different reaction in the clinician, who must be alert to these reactions.
   e. The client has the responsibility to present and clarify the nature of his or her symptoms, reactions to therapy as it progresses, and implement changes suggested in treatment. These areas of responsibility can be complicated by the nature of therapy, which is highly personal and demanding, and by the nature of the client's psychological difficulties, which can interfere with the progress of therapy.
   f. Client's unwillingness to change, financial constraints, refusal by another party to cooperate with therapy, and a variety of practical difficulties in the client's life.

6.

DSM Edition	Goal	Limitations
I	Search for a standard set of diagnostic criteria.	Criteria were vague. Based on unfounded theoretical assumptions.
II	Attempt to use atheoretical concepts that would fit with the ICD system.	Criteria were actually based on psychoanalytic concepts. Criteria were too loose.
III	Precise rating criteria and definitions for each disorder.	Criteria were incompletely specified.
III-R	Further refinement of diagnostic criteria	Became outdated with collection of new research evidence on the disorders.
IV	Incorporation of current research evidence on validity and reliability of diagnoses.	

7. a. The Insanity Defense Reform Act of 1984 had tightened the criteria for a person's psychological disorder to be regarded as grounds for insanity, partly in response to criticisms of the outcome of the John Hinckley case. Further, Dahmer was diagnosed as having a sexual disorder but not a psychotic disorder, unlike Hinckley.
   b. Legislation and judicial rulings regarding the determination of "insanity" focus on whether a person has the capacity to judge the rightness or wrongness of an act, to control his or her impulses to act, and appreciate the wrongfulness of an act.
   c. Determination of competency to stand trial involves predicting whether the defendant will have the cognitive capacity, emotional strength, and freedom from symptoms to make it possible to participate in court proceedings.
   d. Clinicians must determine whether the risk presented by a client to the self or others outweighs the client's right to live independently outside an institution.
   e. Clients are protected by the confidentiality of the clinician-client relationship except when the clinician is obligated to follow through on a "duty to warn" another person about whom the client has expressed harmful intent or in cases where the client might inflict self-harm.
   f. Clients are entitled to provision of psychotherapeutic services, privacy, appropriate clothing, opportunities to interact with other people, to receive and send mail, to use the telephone, to have visitation privileges, comfortable surroundings, exercise, and adequate diet.

MULTIPLE CHOICE

1.	a	6.	d	11.	b	16.	a
2.	c	7.	a	12.	c	17.	d
3.	a	8.	d	13.	b	18.	b
4.	b	9.	a	14.	d	19.	a
5.	c	10	d	15.	b	20.	d

CHAPTER 3
ASSESSMENT

LEARNING OBJECTIVES

1.0 What is a Psychological Assessment?
    1.1 Describe the goals and basic types of assessment procedures.

2.0 Interview
    2.1 Describe the rationale and procedures involved in an unstructured interview.
    2.2 Explain how a structured interview is used in diagnosis, and be familiar with examples such as the SADS, SCID, DIS, and IPDE.

3.0 Mental Status Examination
    3.1 Indicate how appearance and behavior are assessed and why these are important.
    3.2 Describe the methods used to evaluate a client's orientation or awareness of time, place, and identity.
    3.3 Explain the types of disturbance in content of thought.
    3.4 Distinguish the various forms of thought disorders and provide examples.
    3.5 Describe the difference between affect and mood and how they are used in diagnosis.
    3.6 Define the various forms of hallucinations.
    3.7 Explain disturbances in sense of self or identity.
    3.8 Describe how motivation is assessed and its relevance to therapy.
    3.9 Indicate how cognitive deficits and strengths are assessed.
    3.10 Describe the assessment of insight and judgment.

4.0 Psychological Testing
    4.1 Define the concepts of standardization, reliability, and validity.
    4.2 Describe how intelligence is assessed through tests such as the Stanford-Binet Intelligence Test and the Wechsler Intelligence Scales.
    4.3 Explain the role of cultural considerations in the assessment of intelligence.
    4.4 Describe personality and diagnostic tests such as the MMPI-2 and other self-report inventories.
    4.5 Describe projective testing methods such as the Rorschach and the TAT.

5.0 Other Forms of Assessment
    5.1 Indicate how behavioral assessment is used, including self-report and observation.
    5.2 Explain how and why environmental assessments are conducted.
    5.3 Indicate how measures of bodily functioning are used in assessment.
    5.4 Describe psychophysiological measures such as ECG, EMG, GSR, and EEG.
    5.5 Indicate how measures of physical functioning are used in assessment, such as measures of brain structure and function including the CAT scan, MRI, SPECT, and BEAM.
    5.6 Explain the role of neuropsychological assessment and describe measures such as the Halstead-Reitan and Luria-Nebraska.

6.0 Putting It All Together
    6.1 Describe how clinicians use multiple sources of information about a client in putting together a comprehensive assessment.

7.0 Chapter Boxes
    7.1 Outline ethical issues involved in personnel selection.
    7.2 Explain the problems involved in psychological testing of minorities.
    7.3 Indicate the controversies involved in research on intelligence and achievement.

MATCHING

Put the letter from the right-hand column corresponding to the correct match in the blank next to each item in the left-hand column.

1. ____ Altered experience of one's body.
2. ____ Assessment of a client's current functioning in such areas as orientation, thinking style, affect, insight, and motivation.
3. ____ Flow of thoughts that is vague, unfocused, and illogical.
4. ____ Expression of emotion that does not match the nature of the situation.
5. ____ False perception of a sound.
6. ____ Lack of clear sense of who one is.
7. ____ False perception of seeing a person or object.
8. ____ Fabricating facts or events to fill voids in one's memory.
9. ____ Type of test in which test-taker interprets ambiguous stimuli.
10. ____ Behavioral assessment conducted in a specific setting.
11. ____ Experience of losing one's thought in the middle of speaking, leading to a period of silence ranging from seconds to minutes.
12. ____ False perception of a smell.
13. ____ Strength of emotional expression.
14. ____ Type of psychological test comprised of standardized questions with fixed response categories, completed by the test-taker.
15. ____ Thoughts that are odd but not bizarre or deeply entrenched.

a. confabulation
b. blocking
c. auditory hallucination
d. intensity of affect
e. analog observation
f. olfactory hallucination
g. depersonalization
h. overvalued idea
i. self-report clinical inventory
j. mental status examination
k. loosening of associations
l. inappropriate affect
m. identity confusion
n. projective test
o. visual hallucination

IDENTIFYING SYMPTOMS

Write the name of the symptom in the blank next to the behavioral description on the right.

1. _____ Abnormally energized physical activity characterized by rapid movements and speech.
2. _____ Grossly exaggerated conception of one's own importance.
3. _____ Illogical and peculiar connection between objects or events that others see as unrelated.
4. _____ Unpleasant feelings such as sadness or irritability.
5. _____ False belief that one has no money or other material possessions.
6. _____ Abnormally rapid bodily movements involving an obvious level of personal discomfort in which the individual appears to be stirred up.
7. _____ A mood that is neither happy nor sad but shows ordinary day-to-day variations.
8. _____ Erroneous belief that other people are attempting to inflict harm on one.
9. _____ A mood that is more cheerful and elated than average, perhaps even ecstatic.
10. _____ False belief that one's thoughts are being transmitted to others who hear these thoughts.
11. _____ Abnormally slow bodily movements and lethargy.
12. _____ False belief that other people are putting thoughts into one's mind.

IDENTIFYING TESTS

1. Write in the blank next to each test the aspect (or aspects) of functioning it is designed to assess:

I= intelligence   **D=** diagnosis   **H=** physical
P= personality   **S=** psychophysiological   **N=** neuropsychological

a. ____ Stanford-Binet
b. ____ Luria-Nebraska
c. ____ Rorschach
d. ____ IPDE
e. ____ WAIS-R
f. ____ MMPI-2
g. ____ TAT
h. ____ EEG
i. ____ NEO-PI-R
j. ____ Halstead-Reitan
k. ____ CAT scan
l. ____ Bender-Gestalt
m. ____ GSR
n. ____ WISC-III
o. ____ PET scan
p. ____ MRI (or NMR)
q. ____ MCMI-III

LETTER FIND PUZZLE

The following letters are all used in the definitions below. As you fill in each definition, cross out the letters that you have used until there are none left:

```
O  I  Y  S  E  R  T  S  O  A
N  T  D  O  M  C  O  Y  P  N
N  I  I  S  I  S  S  C  U  I
E  T  O  T  D  L  O  E  P  F
O  T  B  N  A  L  M  H  C  N
A  A  S  T  S  A  H  F  L  S
C  O  S  A  N  C  S  U  E  H
I  S  C  E  M  E  N  T  U  A
R  S  O  S  L  I  R  N  T  O
I  P  C  A  N  I  O  I  S  E
```

1. Unwanted repetitive thoughts or images that persist in an individual's consciousness.   _ _ _ _ _ _ _ _ _

2. Deeply entrenched false beliefs that are not consistent with an individual's level of intelligence or cultural background.   _ _ _ _ _ _ _ _

3. Repetitive behaviors that seem to have no purpose, and which are performed in response to a person's uncontrollable urges or according to a ritualistic set of rules.   _ _ _ _ _ _ _ _ _ _ _

4. Disturbance of motor behavior in a psychotic disorder that does not have a physiological cause.   _ _ _ _ _ _ _ _ _

5. Term referring to the "measurement of the mind," and used in describing standards for good psychological tests.   _ _ _ _ _ _ _ _ _ _ _ _

6. A false perception that does not correspond to any objective stimuli in a person's surroundings.   _ _ _ _ _ _ _ _ _ _ _ _

7. Adjective used to describe sadness, used in abnormal psychology to apply to a person's sad mood.   _ _ _ _ _ _ _ _ _

8. An individual's awareness of time, place, and personal identity.   _ _ _ _ _ _ _ _ _ _ _

9. The outward expression of an emotion.   _ _ _ _ _ _

10. Process of evaluating an individual's psychological or physical status.   _ _ _ _ _ _ _ _ _ _

SHORT ANSWER

1. For each of the methods of assessment listed in the chart, describe the procedures involved in the assessment, the advantages of this method, and its disadvantages:

Assessment method	Assessment procedure	Advantages	Disadvantages
Unstructured interview			
Structured interview			
Individual intelligence testing			

Assessment method	Assessment procedure	Advantages	Disadvantages
Self-report clinical inventory			
Projective test			
Behavioral self-report			
Behavioral observation			

2. Answer each of the following questions about the MMPI/MMPI-2:

a. How does the MMPI-2 determine whether a test-taker has falsified responses, been excessively defensive, or been careless in responding?

_____

_____

b. Identify the MMPI-2 scale that is intended to reflect each of the following personality or diagnostic attributes:

_____1) Feelings of unhappiness and low self-esteem

_____2) Asocial and delinquent behaviors

_____3) Elevated mood

_____4) Obsessions, compulsions, and unrealistic fears

_____5) Bodily reactions to stress, denial of psychological problems

_____6) Preoccupation with physical problems and illness

_____7) Bizarre thinking and behavior

c. What was the original intent of the MMPI?

_____

_____

d. How were the MMPI scales developed?

_____

_____

e. Specify three criticisms of the MMPI that the authors of MMPI-2 attempted to address.

_____   _____

f. What five improvements were made in the MMPI-2 in response to criticisms of the MMPI?

_____   _____

_____   _____

3. Answer the following questions about the debate regarding intelligence testing and minorities:

a. What is the main position of *The Bell Curve* by Herrnstein and Murray?

_____

b. What racial differences in intelligence are proposed by Herrnstein and Murray?

_____

c. List three criticisms that have been made of the Herrnstein and Murray position.

_____   _____

_____

4. Identify the types of reliability or validity described in each of the items below:

a. The extent to which two raters agree on how to score a particular response. _____

b. How closely test scores correspond to related measures at that same point in time. _____

c. The degree to which items on a test are correlated with each other. _____

d. How well test scores on one occasion predict performance on other measures at a later occasion. _____

e. General term applying to how closely test scores correspond to other measures with which they are expected to relate. _____

f. The extent to which scores taken on the same test at two different occasions relate to each other. _____

g. How closely a test measures a body of knowledge which it is designed to assess. _____

h. The degree to which a test measures a concept based on a theoretically-derived attribute. _____

5. The following questions relate to the concept and measurement of intelligence:

a. How was the "IQ", or intelligence quotient, originally calculated in the Stanford-Binet measurement of intelligence?

_____

_____

b. How does the "deviation IQ" used in the Wechsler scales differ from the original Stanford-Binet IQ?

_____

_____

c. What three forms of IQ are derived from the Wechsler measures of intelligence?

_____   _____

d. What types of measures are used to assess the three forms of IQ?

_____   _____

e. How do clinicians interpret scores on the Wechsler IQ scales?

_____

_____

MULTIPLE CHOICE

1. Dr. Tobin uses an assessment approach with open-ended questions on reasons for coming to therapy, health symptoms, family background, and life history. This is called a(n):
    a. unstructured interview.
    b. structured interview.
    c. mental status examination.
    d. self-report.

2. A researcher studying depression has each research assistant ask the same questions in the same order to each subject. This is called a(n):
    a. unstructured interview.
    b. structured interview.
    c. mental status examination.
    d. personal history interview.

3. What term would a clinician use to describe a client's understanding and awareness of self and world?
    a. judgment
    b. reactivity
    c. self-monitoring
    d. insight

4. Edward believes that his thoughts, feelings, and behaviors are controlled by the window fan in his room. This symptom is called a:
    a. delusion of control.
    b. visual hallucination.
    c. somatic delusion.
    d. delusion of nihilism.

5. Marnie cannot rid her mind of thoughts of contamination. This symptom is called a(n):
   a. compulsion.
   b. obsession.
   c. thought disorder.
   d. delusion.

6. An assessment method in which the individual rates family or social context is known as a(n):
   a. behavioral observation.
   b. in vivo observation.
   c. behavioral interview.
   d. environmental assessment.

7. A psychologist constructs a measure of "optimism" intended to correlate with other characteristics reflective of optimism. This is known as _____ validity.
   a. construct
   b. criterion
   c. concurrent
   d. content

8. A school psychologist measuring the IQ of a fourth grade boy could administer the:
   a. WAIS-R.
   b. WISC-III.
   c. WPPSI-R.
   d. WBIS.

9. The "mental age" approach used with the Stanford-Binet was abandoned because:
   a. scores were hard to determine for adults.
   b. the term "mental" has a negative meaning.
   c. it did not yield Performance and Verbal IQ.
   d. it was based on a deviation measure of IQ.

10. A clinician concerned about whether or not a client has faked responses on the MMPI-2 would pay careful attention to:
    a. the number of items answered.
    b. the elevation of the clinical scales.
    c. the elevation of the validity scales.
    d. the elevation of the reliability scales.

11. Which test used ambiguous evoked unusual and idiosyncratic responses in the textbook case of Ben Robsham?
    a. Rorschach
    b. MCMI-III
    c. MMPI-2
    d. SCL-90-R

12. A technique for studying the brain involving a computerized combination of x-rays is called:
    a. computerized axial tomography.
    b. magnetic resonance imaging.
    c. nuclear magnetic resonance.
    d. positron emission tomography.

13. A disturbance in thought or the use of language is referred to as a(n)
    a. thought disorder.
    b. illusion.
    c. delusion.
    d. obsession.

14. Dispute over the issue of using personality tests in personnel selection has focused on whether:
    a. test scores should relate to brain scans.
    b. minority applicants may be unfairly judged.
    c. there are no ethical guidelines for their use.
    d. personality tests have no validity.

15. Inconsistency between the person's expression of emotion and the content of speech is called:
    a. mobility of mood.
    b. perseveration.
    c. inappropriateness of affect.
    d. flat affect.

16. A good psychological test is one that follows standardized procedures for scoring and:
    a. diagnosis.
    b. classification.
    c. organization.
    d. administration.

17. What kind of psychological test yields information about cognitive deficits and strengths?
    a. projective test
    b. intelligence test
    c. behavioral assessment
    d. self-report questionnaire

18. Which of the following is the most commonly administered self-report inventory?
    a. Wechsler Adult Intelligence Scale-R
    b. Diagnostic and Statistical Manual of Mental Disorders
    c. Minnesota Multiphasic Personality Inventory
    d. Rorschach Inkblot Test

19. Dr. Schwartz asks his client to keep a tally of the number of times per hour he says negative things to his wife. This assessment technique is:
   a. behavioral interviewing.
   b. self-actualization keying.
   c. self-monitoring.
   d. behavioral observation.

20. Which of the following is an assessment measure specifically designed for use with individuals from diverse cultural and ethnic backgrounds?
   a. NEO-PI-R
   b. SCORS
   c. WISC-III
   d. SOMPA

ANSWERS

MATCHING
1. g	6. m	11. b	
2. j	7. o	12. f	
3. k	8. a	13. d	
4. l	9. n	14. i	
5. c	10. e	15. h	

IDENTIFYING SYMPTOMS
1. hyperactivity
2. delusion of grandeur
3. magical thinking
4. dysphoric mood
5. delusion of poverty
6. psychomotor agitation
7. normal or euthymic mood
8. delusion of persecution
9. euphoric mood
10. thought broadcasting
11. psychomotor retardation
12. thought insertion

IDENTIFYING TESTS
1. a. I	e. I	i. P	m. S
b. N	f. D+P	j. N	n. I
c. P	g. P	k. H	o. H
d. D	h. S	l. N	p. H
			q. D+P

LETTER FIND PUZZLE
1. OBSESSIONS
2. DELUSIONS
3. COMPULSION
4. CATATONIA
5. PSYCHOMETRICS
6. HALLUCINATION
7. DYSPHORIC
8. ORIENTATION
9. AFFECT
10. ASSESSMENT

SHORT ANSWER
1.

Assessment method	Assessment procedure	Advantages	Disadvantages
Unstructured interview	Open-ended questions about personal and family history, symptoms, and reasons for seeking treatment.	Flexibility allows interviewer to adapt questions and questioning style to client's responses.	Variation from interviewer to interviewer in nature of questions. Skill and experience are necessary.
Structured interview	Highly structured set of questions with predetermined wording and order.	No extensive knowledge of inter-viewing techniques required. Standardized ratings based on research criteria can be obtained.	None are stated in text.

Assessment method	Assessment procedure	Advantages	Disadvantages
Individual intelligence testing	Standardized questions that tap different verbal and nonverbal abilities.	Rich qualitative information about the client's thought processes and judgment.	Cultural bias. Lack of clear support for validity of test scores in terms of relation to behaviors in everyday life.
Self-report clinical inventory	Standardized questions with fixed response categories that test-taker completes on his or her own.	Are "objective" in that scoring does not require judgment by clinician. Can be given to large numbers of people.	Questions are "subjective" in that they often have a theoretical basis, and interpretation of scores can be affected by clinician's biases.
Projective test	Test-taker is presented with ambiguous item or task and asked to "project" his or her own meaning onto it.	Assumed to tap unconscious determinants of personality.	Difficulties in establishing reliability and validity.
Behavioral self-report	Behavioral interviews, self-monitoring, and check list.	Detailed information about symptoms, goals for intervention, and basis for evaluation.	Difficult for client to report certain behaviors. Detailed background information is hard to obtain.
Behavioral observation	In vivo or analog observations of the target behavior(s).	Avoids the problem of clients attempting to present themselves in a favorable light on self-report measures.	Observations affect the people whose behavior is being observed.

2. a. There are three validity scales that ascertain how defensive the test-taker was, and also whether the individual may have been careless, confused, or intentionally lying.
    b. 1) Depression (2); 2) Psychopathic deviate (4); 3) Hypomania (9); 4) Psychasthenia (7); 5) Hysteria (3); 6) Hypochondriasis (1); 7) Schizophrenia (8).
    c. To provide an assessment device that was efficient to administer and score, and could be used for the purposes of objectively arriving at diagnoses of psychological disorders (a "cookbook") .
    d. The procedure of "empirical criterion keying" was used. Items developed by the test authors were administered to psychiatric patients and to non-psychiatric hospital patients and others. Items on which these groups differed and which were sensitive to psychiatric diagnosis were included in the final scales of the MMPI.
    e. The comparison group of "normals" did not reflect the population diversity of the U.S.
        Many items were outdated or offensive by current standards.
        The psychometric data in support of the MMPI were only moderate.
    f. A more representative sample was used to collect data on normal individuals as well as on psychiatric patients.
        The items were brought up-to-date.
        Subcultural biases were eliminated.
        More subtle validity scales were included.
        Additional personality assessment scales were included.

3. a. Intelligence is a heritable trait that predicts and possibly causes a variety of social outcomes, including social attainment or failure of the individual as well as problems for society as a whole.
   b. Higher overall IQ's for Asians compared to whites and blacks; higher IQ's for whites compared to blacks.
   c. There is considerable evidence for environmental contributions to intelligence.
      Intelligence may be a multifaceted trait, and tests of intelligence do not take all abilities into account.
      The definition of distinct races is difficult to make.

4. a. interjudge reliability   c. internal consistency   e. criterion validity   g. content validity
   b. concurrent validity   d. predictive validity   f. test-retest reliability   h. construct validity

5. a. IQ was originally calculated as the ratio of "mental age" to "chronological age."
   b. The deviation IQ is based on conversion of a person's actual test score to a score that reflects how high or low the score compares to the scores of others in that person's age and gender group.
   c. Verbal IQ
      Performance IQ
      Full Scale IQ
   d. Verbal IQ: vocabulary, factual knowledge, short-term memory, and verbal reasoning.
      Performance IQ: psychomotor abilities, nonverbal reasoning, and ability to learn new relationships.
      Full Scale IQ: the total of scores on both the Verbal and Performance IQ measures.
   e. Scores on the Wechsler scales are interpreted by clinicians by referring to published guidelines and by formulating a picture of the client's cognitive strengths and weaknesses on the basis of how the test-taker responded to particular items and the test situation in general. The interpretation must also take into account a person's background, especially when that person's background does not match those on whom the test was standardized..

MULTIPLE CHOICE

1. a	6. d	11. a	16. d
2. b	7. a	12. a	17. b
3. d	8. b	13. a	18. c
4. a	9. a	14. b	19. c
5. b	10. c	15. c	20. d

CHAPTER 4
PSYCHODYNAMIC AND HUMANISTIC PERSPECTIVES

LEARNING OBJECTIVES

1.0 The Purpose of Theories in Abnormal Psychology
   1.1 Describe the purpose of theories as the basis for understanding and treating abnormal behavior.
2.0 Psychodynamic Perspective
   2.1 Describe the main concepts of Freud's theory, including the structure of personality, psychodynamics, defense mechanisms, stages of psychosexual development, and Freud's place in history.
   2.2 Describe the theories of other psychodynamic theorists, including Jung, Adler, Horney, Erikson, Sullivan, and the object relations theorists.
   2.3 Explain the essential features of Freudian psychoanalysis and differentiate this form of therapy from other psychodynamic treatments.
   2.4 Describe the theoretical criticisms of Freud's work, research on the role of psychosocial factors and attachment in early personality development, and the growth of new therapeutic models.
3.0 Humanistic Perspective
   3.1 Explain the main concepts of the person-centered approach of Rogers.
   3.2 Outline the main features of Maslow's self-actualization theory.
   3.3 Describe treatment based on the humanistic perspective.
   3.4 Indicate how humanistic theories have contributed to education, industry, and the provision of psychotherapy.
4.0 Chapter Boxes
   4.1 Outline the controversy regarding the issue of repressed memories.
   4.2 Describe feminist approaches to psychotherapy and how they contrast with traditional psychoanalysis.
   4.3 Explain how research on subliminal activation contributes to the understanding of the role of the unconscious in personality dynamics.

MATCHING

Put the letter from the right-hand column corresponding to the correct match in the blank next to each item in the left-hand column.

1. ___ The ego's logical and rational style of thinking.
2. ___ Freud's proposed view of the basis of feminine psychology.
3. ___ Method used by psychoanalysts to encourage clients to talk openly about their unconscious thought processes.
4. ___ Stage of development in Freud's theory in which the infant experiences hostile urges toward caregivers.
5. ___ What Adler and Horney regard as the attempt by a maladjusted individual to avoid facing the weaknesses of the real self.
6. ___ Object relations theorist who emphasized the infant's fantasy life.
7. ___ What Rogers called the optimally adjusted individual.
8. ___ Psychological process that is characterized by a lack of gratification, according to Maslow.
9. ___ English psychologist who criticized psychoanalysis as ineffective.
10. ___ The process in Freud's theory in which young child feels romantic love toward the opposite-sex parent.
11. ___ The id's distorted cognitive representation of the world.
12. ___ Researcher who developed the "Strange Situation" to study attachment processes in infants.

a. free association
b. Oedipal complex
c. Hans Eysenck
d. primary process thinking
e. fully-functioning person
f. Mary Ainsworth
g. conditions of worth
h. rapprochement
i. secondary process thinking
j. seduction hypothesis
k. oral-aggressive phase
l. penis envy
m. Melanie Klein
n. neurotic excuses
o. deficit need

13. ___ According to Rogers, parental communications that cause children to feel they are loved only if certain demands are fulfilled.
14. ___ Interpretation rejected by Freud that the patients with hysteria he treated were victims of incest.
15. ___ According to Mahler, the most important phase of development.

IDENTIFYING THEORIES

Put the letter corresponding to the theoretical perspective in the blank next to the concept.

F= Freudian psychoanalysis
P= Post-Freudian psychodynamic (Jung, Adler, Horney, Erikson, and Sullivan)
O= Object relations (Klein, Winnicot, Kohut, Mahler)
H= Humanistic (Rogers and Maslow)

Perspective   Concept
1. ____ Neurosis results from the individual's misguided efforts to live up to the image of the idealized self.
2. ____ Psychological disorder results from defects in the self created by faulty parenting.
3. ____ Personality continues to develop throughout life in a series of psychosocial "crises."
4. ____ Psychologically healthy people boost their feelings of well-being by their ability to have peak experiences.
5. ____ Fantasized images in infancy of parents as "good" and "bad" form the basis of the later development of the self.
6. ____ Severe psychological disturbance is the result of faulty communication patterns learned in early life.
7. ____ Psychological disorder is the result of id-ego-superego imbalances.
8. ____ The deepest layer of the unconscious mind is made up of archetypal images representing universal human themes.
9. ____ Psychological disturbance results from incongruence between one's self-concept and one's experiences.
10.____ Unconscious sexual and aggressive impulses provide the fundamental motivation for human behavior.

MIND BOGGLE PUZZLE

Each box below contains a term that is defined in the clue below it. The letters of the term are connected to each other in the box, but they may follow any direction. Indicate your answer by drawing a line connecting the letters in the box.

S U G S C I J P N K Q E G E R Y C V E I P X G O W	B C O X F G P N G R H J T Y U A Q O R E T V E C N	C R F H J L A Q W S U C T X M P O E N B Z Y P C Y	Y E X V Q S B I S T C W M N E O Q T H J V I A L P	T R B W E X V A N X I U E F S N E R O C C E K H G
The structure of personality that, according to Freud, contains the conscience and the ego-ideal.	Term used by Rogers to describe a psychological state in which an individual's self-concept is consistent with experiences.	Psychosexual development stage in late childhood in which sexual urges become relatively unimportant forces in personality.	Theory in psychology that emphasizes living each moment to the fullest.	Process in psychotherapy in which the client carries over feelings toward parents onto the therapist.

SHORT ANSWER

1. Match the theorist with the concept:

Theorist	Concept
___ a. Freud	1. psychosocial crisis
___ b. Jung	2. narcissism
___ c. Adler	3. hierarchy of needs
___ d. Horney	4. idealized self
___ e. Erikson	5. person-centered
___ f. Sullivan	6. problems in living
___ g. Winnicott	7. separation-individuation
___ h. Kohut	8. social interest
___ i. Mahler	9. transitional object
___ j. Rogers	10. libido
___ k. Maslow	11. archetypes

2. For each of the theorists indicated below, summarize their position on the role of early parenting on the healthy development of the self and the development of psychological disorder:

Theorist	Healthy development	Psychological disorder
Sullivan		
Kohut		
Mahler		
Rogers		

3. Describe the contributions, criticisms, and type of research associated with each of the theoretical perspectives below:

Perspective	Contributions	Criticisms	Current evaluation
Psychoanalytic			
Psychodynamic (Post-Freudian)			
Humanistic			

4. For each of the theorists below, summarize the goals of treatment and approach or approaches used in therapy:

Theorist	Goals of treatment	Approach in therapy
Freud		
Adler		
Horney		
Erikson		
Sullivan		
Object relations theorists		
Rogers		

5. The following behaviors are examples of each of the ego defense mechanisms identified in Freudian theory. In the blank to the left of each example, name the defense mechanism it represents:

a. _____ Asserting that alcohol is not a problem in one's life even though one drinks heavily.
b. _____ A person is angry with a roommate and intentionally breaks a glass.
c. _____ After being turned down by a prospective dating partner, a person goes to her room and sulks.
d. _____ A student fails a test and falsely attributes the failure to feeling ill.
e. _____ A daughter insists that she "hates" her mother completely after her mother refuses to lend her money.
f. _____ One mentally relives a tragic situation and makes it come out all right.
g. _____ A soccer player talks about her painful knee operation in a detached and impersonal way.
h. _____ A student forgets about the time he made a fool out of himself at a friend's party.
i. _____ A woman is excessively nice to an acquaintance about whom she is acutely jealous.
j _____ Someone wrongly accuses a person to whom she is attracted of flirting with her.

6. Write in the blanks the psychosexual stage with which each characteristic is most closely associated:
O=oral   A=anal   P=phallic   G=genital

___ a. Smoking
___ b. Being unusually tidy
___ c. Failing to establish a stable career
___ d. Being sarcastic
___ e. Having overly sloppy living habits
___ f. Holding extremely harsh standards of moralistic behavior
___ g. Unable to share in romantic relationships
___ h. Failing to establish a sense of morality

7. Answer the following questions about the Research Focus on Subliminal Activation:
a. What was the main hypothesis of Silverman's work?

_____

b. What procedure did Silverman use to test this hypothesis?

_____

c. Why is the procedure called "subliminal activation?"

_____

d. What was the "experimental" condition in this research?

_____

e. What was the "control" condition?

_____

f. The dependent measure in this research was:

_____

g. What types of experimental populations have been tested with the subliminal activation method?

_____

h. What are the controversies and limitations of Silverman's experiments?

_____
_____
_____

8. Indicate in the blank next to each item which aspect of Maslow's theory it pertains to using the following codes:

P= Peak experiences   **H**= Hierarchy of needs   **S**= Self-actualization:

a. ___ The fulfillment of security needs before the fulfillment of self-esteem needs.

b. ___ Feeling a tremendous surge of inner happiness and harmony with the outside world.

c. ___ The need for physical comfort and safety take priority over reading a good book.

d. ___ Feeling that one can accept one's own weaknesses.

e. ___ Liking people without having to approve of what they do.

f. ___ Achieving a strong sense of spiritual fulfillment.

g. ___ Having a sense of purpose or mission in life.

h. ___ Feeling loved enough by others to go on and seek ways to improve one's self-understanding.

BONUS PUZZLE

This is an "acrostic" puzzle in which the letters in the clues, when rearranged, form a quotation. The clues are common words, and when you put the letter in each clue in the numbered space in the puzzle, the quote will contain Sigmund Freud's perspective on the use of dreams in understanding personality:

Sound made by a lion.

$\overline{1}\ \overline{18}\ \overline{8}\ \overline{6}$

What you do when you say "One, two, three ....."

$\overline{17}\ \overline{2}\ \overline{24}\ \overline{19}\ \overline{12}$

Sodium hydroxide (rhymes with "pie").

$\overline{5}\ \overline{3}\ \overline{14}$

Sound made by an owl.

$\overline{13}\ \overline{7}\ \overline{23}\ \overline{10}$

The opposite of happy.

$\overline{25}\ \overline{4}\ \overline{9}$

Son of your aunt and uncle.

$\overline{21}\ \overline{11}\ \overline{15}\ \overline{20}\ \overline{22}\ \overline{16}$

1	2	3	4	5		6	7	8	9		10	11		12	13	14		15	16	17	18	19	20	21	22	23	24	25

MULTIPLE CHOICE

1. Freud's statement that "the child is father to the man" means that:
   a. early life experiences play a formative role in the development of personality.
   b. children are often more psychologically healthy than adults.
   c. adults can learn a great deal by observing the behavior of children.
   d. resolution of the Oedipal conflict is needed for healthy adult functioning.

2. Id is to ego as:
   a. instinct is to conscience.
   b. secondary is to primary process thinking.
   c. pleasure principle is to reality principle.
   d. ego is to superego.

3. According to Freudian theory, the ego's energy is derived from:
   a. secondary process thinking.
   b. the decision making abilities of the ego.
   c. the dictates of the superego.
   d. the energy of the id.

4. As discussed in the Critical Issue on "repressed" memories of early childhood abuse:
   a. memory of early life events is highly accurate and reliable.
   b. adults accused of abuse confess to their behavior when confronted.
   c. children's memories are not necessarily accurate and are subject to distortion.
   d. clinicians agree that such memories should not be discussed in therapy

5. According to Freudian theory, which behavior would suggest fixation at the anal stage?
   a. compulsive pursuit of gratification.
   b. a drive to "work and love."
   c. hostility and a critical attitude.
   d. rigid over-control and hoarding.

6. Every time that Alyssa enters her therapist's office, she feels anxious and apprehensive, feelings similar to her fearful reactions to her father. Psychodynamic theorists would call this response:
   a. transference.
   b. countertransference.
   c. resistance.
   d. a defense mechanism.

7. The Q-sort was used by Carl Rogers to measure:
   a. incongruence between actual and ideal self.
   b. incongruence between actual and real self.
   c. degree of an individual's self-actualization.
   d. an individual's capacity for empathy.

8. Which theorist conceptualized a pyramid-like structure called the hierarchy of needs specifying the order in which human needs must be fulfilled?
   a. Mahler
   b. Laing
   c. Maslow
   d. Rogers

9. Existential theorists believe that:
   a. it is important to appreciate fully each moment as it occurs.
   b. fundamental flaws in human nature cause psychological disorders.
   c. unconscious factors are the basis of human behavior and existence.
   d. human existence represents a continual struggle between good and evil.

10. What is the term for the phase of psychodynamic treatment in which the client is helped to achieve a healthier resolution of earlier childhood issues?
    a. transference
    b. working through
    c. dream analysis
    d. free association

11. What is the term in psychoanalytic theory that refers to an individual's personal model of all that is exemplary in life?
    a. superego
    b. ego
    c. ego-ideal
    d. alter ego

12. Feminist-relational approaches to therapy emphasize which themes?
    a. the need of the client to establish herself independently of her relationships
    b. the client's need to understand her relationships in terms of penis envy
    c. the relationship between the client's physical and psychological symptoms
    d. the client's feelings about significant relationships and connections in her life

13. Which of the following statements best characterizes current thinking regarding the theoretical perspective that should be assumed by a clinician?
    a. Clinicians typically adopt one perspective from which to treat all individuals.
    b. Most clinicians tend to identify with one perspective but borrow from other perspectives when appropriate.
    c. Most clinicians view the psychodynamic perspective as outdated and therefore utilize the humanistic perspective.
    d. Currently, most clinicians are disillusioned by the psychological perspectives and have adopted the medical perspective.

14. When defense mechanisms are used in a rigid or extreme fashion, they become the source of:
    a. adjustment.
    b. psychological disorders.
    c. ego strength.
    d. unconscious impulses.

15. Each of Freud's psychosexual stages centers around:
    a. the mother-infant bond.
    b. one of the body's erogenous zones.
    c. psychosocial crises in childhood.
    d. development of adequate defense mechanisms.

16. Which post-Freudian theorist postulated that each individual progresses through a life-long set of eight crises?
    a. Adler
    b. Horney
    c. Erikson
    d. Sullivan

17. The concept of the "therapeutic community" was developed by which post-Freudian?
    a. Mahler
    b. Sullivan
    c. Adler
    d. Winnicott

18. George's psychoanalyst is urging him to sit back, relax, and say whatever is on his mind. This technique is known as:
    a. dream analysis.
    b. free association.
    c. client centering.
    d. word association.

19. According to Sullivan, what role does the clinician play in improving the client's interpersonal problems?
    a. actor-observer
    b. facilitator
    c. participant observer
    d. objective analyst

20. To counteract the conditions of worth a person experienced in childhood, Rogers believed that clients should be treated with

    _____.
    a. sympathy
    b. unconditional positive regard
    c. courtesy
    d. dream analysis

ANSWERS
MATCHING

1. i	6. m	11. d
2. l	7. e	12. f
3. a	8. o	13. g
4. k	9. c	14. j
5. n	10. b	15. h

IDENTIFYING THEORIES

1. P (Adler and Horney)	4. H (Maslow)	7. F
2. O	5. O (Klein)	8. P (Jung)
3. P (Erikson)	6. P (Sullivan)	9. H (Rogers)
		10. F

MIND BOGGLE PUZZLE
SUPEREGO
CONGRUENCE
LATENCY
EXISTENTIAL
TRANSFERENCE

SHORT ANSWER

1.
   - a. 10
   - b. 11
   - c. 8
   - d. 4
   - e. 1
   - f. 6
   - g. 9
   - h. 2
   - i. 7
   - j. 5
   - k. 3

2.

Theorist	Healthy development	Psychological disorder
Sullivan	Caregiver who is calm and non-anxious communicates to her child feelings of nurturance and reassurance. The child is able to develop without having to cope with feelings of anxiety.	An anxious caregiver communicates to her child her own anxiety, causing the child, in turn, to experience anxiety. The child's feelings of anxiety interfere with the ability to learn appropriate ways of communicating in thought and language.
Kohut	Parents communicate to the child their pride in the child's accomplishments, which helps the child develop a favorable sense of self-esteem.	Child develops a disturbed sense of self as a result of parents who fail to show their pride and approval in the child's activities.
Mahler	Infant develops through phases in which an autonomous self develops; healthy development results when the caregiver establishes an appropriate balance between supporting dependence and independence.	Disturbance in the sense of self results from being raised by a caregiver who fails to provide adequate nurturance or does not support the child's establishment of autonomy.
Rogers	Parents who help the child feel accepted for who the child is promote healthy self-development and congruence between self and experiences.	When parents establish conditions of worth, the child feels loved only when certain demands are fulfilled. This situation ultimately leads to the development of incongruence.

3.

Perspective	Contributions	Criticisms	Current evaluation
Psychoanalytic	First modern psychological theory. First systematic approach to psychological disorder. First approach to emphasize psychological causes of disturbed behavior. Emphasized importance of the unconscious.	Difficult to test empirically. Difficult to disprove on logical grounds. Negative view of women in idea of penis envy. Freud's rejection of seduction hypothesis may have been motivated by political reasons. Traditional psychoanalysis is ineffective.	Some supportive evidence in experimental studies of unconscious processes. Brief therapy make it possible to evaluate therapeutic interventions in controlled studies. Freud's theory now viewed increasingly in terms of the context in which it was developed.

Perspective	Contributions	Criticisms	Current evaluation
Psychodynamic (Post-Freudian)	Incorporated into psychological theory the importance of cognitive processes, interpersonal relations, and social factors. Many important ideas introduced by individual theorists. Expanded psychotherapy beyond psychoanalysis.	Many concepts are as difficult to test experimentally. Evidence to support theories biased by the nature of the methods used to collect the evidence.	Large number of research studies have supported the ideas of these theorists, including research on Erikson's theory, Adler, and attachment styles.
Humanistic	More positive view of human behavior than that offered by psychodynamic perspective. Widespread influence of humanistic ideas has occurred throughout psychology.	Methods of therapy rely heavily on self-report, making them inappropriate for certain disorders. Downplays role of the unconscious and may therefore be overly simplistic. Given the nature of disorders which the perspective can explain, there is a narrow range of clients for whom therapy is appropriate.	Maslow's theory not well-supported by research. Applications of Maslow to business and industry not widely supported. Emphasis by Rogers on research using the Q-sort, and factors affecting therapy outcome give the theory an empirical base and support the importance of empathy.

4.

Theory	Goals of treatment	Approach in therapy
Freud	Bring into conscious awareness the individual's unconscious conflicts.	Free association. Dream analysis. Analysis of transference issues. Interpretation of resistance.
Adler	Help the individual lead a more productive life.	Collaboration between client and therapist to examine client's feelings of inferiority and boost sense of inner confidence.
Horney	Help the individual regain lost connections to the inner self.	Help client explore unrealistic demands imposed by the idealized self's expectations, and instead accept the flawed, but "true" self.
Erikson	Achieve more favorable resolutions of psychosocial crises.	Help client discover factors impeding the individual's successful resolution of the psychosocial crisis.
Sullivan	Help client overcome interpersonal problems through developing improved communication.	Clinician becomes a "participant observer" who actively tries to correct client's ineffective patterns of interactions with other people. Build the client's sense of security so that client feels less threatened by rejection from other people in the client's life.

Theory	Goals of treatment	Approach in therapy
Object relations theorists	Reverse destructive processes that occurred early in the client's life.	Through good "parenting," the therapist tries to restore the client's sense of self and control over the self's boundaries. Empathy in therapeutic relationship helps client feel appreciated and accepted as individual (Kohut).
Rogers	Help clients discover their inherent goodness. Achieve greater self-understanding.	Provide unconditional positive regard. Use empathy to see client's situation as it appears to the client. Reflection and clarification of client's feelings and thoughts. Provide model of genuineness and willingness to self-disclose.

5. a. denial   e. splitting   h. repression
    b. displacement f. undoing   i. reaction
    c. regression   g. isolation of   formation
    d. rationalization   affect   j. projection

6. a. oral   e. anal
    b. anal   f. phallic
    c. genital g. genital
    d. oral   h. phallic

7. a. Silverman hypothesized that unconscious conflict underlies psychological symptoms.
    b. The procedure used to test this hypothesis involved presenting words on a tachistoscope on which they could be presented to subjects in rapid succession.
    c. The method is called "subliminal activation" because it is assumed that words presented just below conscious awareness are processed at an unconscious level.
    d. The experimental condition involved presenting phrases that were intended to stimulate unconscious libidinal messages to the subjects, with words that had aggressive, sexual, or fantasy content.
    e. In the control condition, subjects were presented with words or phrases that were intended to have neutral content.
    f. Response time to read the phrases served as the dependent measure.
    g. The subject populations have included people with schizophrenia, homosexual men, depressed persons, and smokers.
    h. The control condition is not a true control condition, as the supposedly "neutral" words could have unconscious meanings to certain individuals.
    There is debate about whether the unconscious conflicts presumably activated by the method actually have relevance for the subjects, each of whom has his or her own unique psychological history and makeup.

8. a. H   e. S   **BONUS PUZZLE**
    b. P   f. P   ROAR
    c. H   g. S   COUNT   FINAL ANSWER: "ROYAL ROAD TO THE
    d. S   h. H   LYE   UNCONSCIOUS"
                    HOOT
                    SAD
                    COUSIN

MULTIPLE CHOICE

1. a   6. a   11. c   16. c
2. c   7. a   12. d   17. b
3. d   8. c   13. b   18. b
4. c   9. a   14. b   19. c
5. d   10 b   15. b   20. b

CHAPTER 5
FAMILY SYSTEMS, BEHAVIORAL, AND BIOLOGICAL PERSPECTIVES

LEARNING OBJECTIVES

1.0 Family Systems Perspective
    1.1 Describe how faulty communication patterns such as paradoxical communication are thought to contribute to the development of psychological disorders within family members.
    1.2 Explain how disturbed family structures such as parent-child alliances and enmeshed families can lead to symptoms in individuals within families.
    1.3 Indicate how the factors within a family system can create and maintain psychological disorders.
    1.4 Outline the methods of family therapy, including paradoxical interventions.
    1.5 Describe the limitations of research supporting the family systems approach and the more favorable evidence regarding the effectiveness of family therapy.

2.0 Behavioral Perspective
    2.1 Explain how principles of classical conditioning have been applied to analysis of the causes of psychological disorder.
    2.2 Distinguish operant conditioning from classical conditioning and show how the principle of reinforcement can be applied to understanding the development of symptoms.
    2.3 Describe the social learning and social cognitive approaches to psychological disorder, including the more recent focus of this approach on self-efficacy.
    2.4 Indicate how cognitive-behavioral theories account for psychological disorders, and how faulty cognitions are seen as the cause of emotional distress.
    2.5 Differentiate the behavioral forms of treatment including conditioning techniques such as counterconditioning and desensitization, assertiveness training, contingency management, modeling and self-efficacy training, cognitive-behavioral therapy, and behavioral medicine.
    2.6 Describe the evidence in support of the effectiveness of behavioral approaches to treatment.

3.0 Biological Perspective
    3.1 Outline the structure and functions within the central nervous system, the neuron and synapse, neurotransmitters, the structures within the brain, and the autonomic nervous system.
    3.2 Describe the role of the endocrine system in behavior, including the effect of hormones.
    3.3 Explain basic concepts in genetics, such as genes, chromosomes, genotype, and phenotype.
    3.4 Indicate the major models of genetic transmission of inherited traits and diseases.
    3.5 Outline the forms of biologically-based therapies, including medication and somatic treatments such as psychosurgery.
    3.6 Describe the search for genetic causes of psychological disorder and the current status of research findings.

4.0 Developing a Perspective: An Integrative Approach
    4.1 Explain how integrative models of psychotherapy put together the concepts and methods of the major perspectives in abnormal psychology.

5.0 Chapter Boxes
    5.1 Describe the ethical and practical dilemmas involved in genetic counseling.
    5.1 Explain how changes in families due to divorce can create potential psychological difficulties for children as they grow up.
    5.3 Indicate how cognitive-behavioral treatments have been applied to the treatment of sex offenders.

MATCHING

Put the letter from the right-hand column corresponding to the correct match in the blank next to each item in the left-hand column.

1. ___ The learning of an association between a neutral stimulus and a behavior that usually occurs reflexively.
2. ___ System in the body involved in controlling automatic, involuntary processes necessary for survival.
3. ___ Brain region involved in controlling balance and motor coordination.
4. ___ Part of the neuron that transmits information to other neurons.
5. ___ Form of behavioral treatment in which a client receives rewards for performing desired behaviors and not for performing undesired behaviors.
6. ___ System in the body containing the brain and spinal cord.
7. ___ Treatment method in family therapy in which a family is instructed to interact in problematic ways.
8. ___ Type of learning in which individual acquires new behaviors by being reinforced for performing them.
9. ___ Part of the cortex involved in abstract planning and judgment.
10. ___ Area of the neuron that receives neural transmissions.
11. ___ Assumptions or personal rules that interfere with an individual's adjustment.
12. ___ Method of therapy in which a person's negative assumptions and ideas are reframed in more positive ways.
13. ___ Point of communication between two or more neurons.
14. ___ Unit of inheritance on which genes are located.
15. ___ Chemical substance produced by endocrine glands.

a. cognitive restructuring
b. operant conditioning
c. central nervous system
d. dysfunctional attitudes
e. synapse
f. classical conditioning
g. paradoxical intervention
h. prefrontal cortex
i. synaptic terminal
j. contingency management
k. hormone
l. dendrite
m. basal ganglia
n. autonomic nervous system
o. chromosome

IDENTIFYING THE CONCEPT

Indicate which theoretical perspective is represented by each of these concepts:

Perspectives

BI= Biological
FS= Family systems
CB= Cognitive-behavioral
BE= Behavioral
SL= Social learning

Perspective	Concept	Perspective	Concept
1. _____	Double bind	8. _____	Shaping
2. _____	Automatic thought	9. _____	Identified patient
3. _____	A-B-C model	10. _____	Reticular formation
4. _____	Extinction	11. _____	Generalization
5. _____	Concordance rate	12. _____	Cross-fostering
6. _____	Vicarious reinforcement	13. _____	Self-efficacy
7. _____	Penetrance	14. _____	Heritability

SHORT ANSWER

1. Match the name of the theorist or researcher with the concept that he introduced to psychology.

Name		Concept	
___ Meichenbaum	___ Wolpe	1. irrational beliefs	6. self-efficacy
___ Watson	___ Skinner	2. counterconditioning	7. operant conditioning
___ Bandura	___ Bateson	3. classical conditioning	8. stress inoculation training
___ Minuchin	___ Pavlov	4. paradoxical communication	9. enmeshed families
___ Ellis		5. conditioned fear	

2. Place an "X" next to the term or name that does not belong with the others:

a. token economy
    systematic desensitization
    counterconditioning
    cognitive restructuring

c. discrimination
    modeling
    vicarious reinforcement
    expectancies

e. criticism
    food
    money
    praise

b. amygdala
    corpus callosum
    pituitary gland
    cerebellum

d. Bateson
    Beck
    Meichenbaum
    Ellis

f. genotype
    phenotype
    polygenic model
    biofeedback

3. Describe the main points, criticisms, and current evaluation of each of the theoretical perspectives below:

Perspective	Underlying assumption about the causes of psychological disorder	Current evaluation
Family systems		
Behavioral (conditioning models)		
Social learning		
Cognitive-behavioral		
Biological		

4. For each of the theoretical perspectives listed below summarize the goals of treatment approaches used in therapy:

Theory	Goals of treatment	Approach in therapy
Family systems		
Behavioral (conditioning models)		
Social learning		
Cognitive-behavioral		
Biological		

5. As a child, Sandy became terrified when she almost fell out of a fast-moving roller coaster. Now as an adult, Sandy feels panicky when she takes her children to a park or fair where there is a roller coaster. Apply the terms from the classical conditioning model of Pavlov to Sandy's experience:

Unconditioned stimulus_____   Unconditioned response _____

Conditioned stimulus _____   Conditioned response _____

6. Answer the following questions about research on the genetic causes of psychological disorder:
a. How is concordance rate determined?

_____

b. Why is reliance on a concordance rate incomplete as far as providing a basis for determining genetic contributions to disorders?

_____

c. What is the advantage of conducting an adoption study compared to determining the concordance rate of a disorder?

_____

d. What is the major advantage of conducting a cross-fostering adoption study?

_____

PSYCH-TAC-TOE
_____

Try to answer all the questions in the squares without referring to the answers. Then, when you have answered as many as you can, check the answers, which will be labelled "X" and "O". See if you made "Tic-tac-toe" by drawing in the X's and O's for each right answer.

The basic unit of heredity.	The stimulus that causes a reflexive response before any learning has taken place.	Rate at which reinforcements are provided.
Behavioral training method in which client learns to behave in a less intimidated manner.	Part of the brain involved in short-term memory.	Concepts a person uses to view the world and the self.
Interpersonal messages that communicate contradictory information.	Genetic disease that causes progressive deterioration of the central nervous system, involuntary muscle contractions, personality change, dementia, and ultimately death.	Basic unit of structure and function in the nervous system.

MULTIPLE CHOICE

1. The family perspective was developed in the late 1960s within the emerging framework of:
   a. humanistic theory.
   b. systems theory.
   c. behavioral theory.
   d. integrative theory.

2. Jonathan tells his college-age son that he wants him to take more responsibility for personal finances, but then scolds him for opening up his own checking account. Jonathan's interaction with is son exemplifies which kind of communication?
   a. double bind
   b. paradoxical
   c. enmeshed
   d. systemic

3. "Systemic" is to Haley as "Structural" is to:
   a. Bateson.
   b. Erikson.
   c. Minuchin.
   d. Milan.

4. In couples therapy, Aileen and her husband are instructed by the therapist to try to argue more frequently. What is the term for this therapeutic technique?
   a. systemic intervention
   b. structural intervention
   c. paradoxical communication
   d. paradoxical intervention

5. Parental divorce is most likely to have negative effects on children when:
   a. parental conflict is high before, during, and after the divorce.
   b. family income rises following the divorce.
   c. the parents give too much attention to the child.
   d. the divorce occurs during the child's infant years.

6. In Skinner's view of Utopia, what was the main basis for promoting socialization and human development?
   a. negative reinforcement
   b. positive reinforcement
   c. primary reinforcers
   d. secondary reinforcers

7. On several occasions Harry has been inspired to speak up at staff meetings by observing the success of his boss acting assertively. In social learning terms, this situation exemplifies:
   a. situational generalization.
   b. primary reinforcement.
   c. secondary reinforcement.
   d. vicarious reinforcement.

8. According to Ellis, emotional disturbance arises when an individual has:
   a. early life experiences involving inordinate amounts of punishment.
   b. views about the self and the world that are unrealistic, extreme, and illogical.
   c. automatic thoughts and dysfunctional attitudes.
   d. personal constructs that are out of touch with reality.

9. Marta has sought therapy because of her tendency to feel anxious and intimidated in situations in which she should be able to express justifiable anger. Marta's therapist tells her that the therapy, which is based on Wolpe's technique of counterconditioning, is known as:
   a. cognitive restructuring.
   b. assertiveness training.
   c. systematic desensitization.
   d. contingency management.

10. The technical name for the "master gland" is the:
    a. pituitary gland.
    b. hypothalamus.
    c. limbic system.
    d. brain.

11. Cognitive-behavioral treatment of sex offenders involves which of the following procedures?
    a. insisting that they admit to feelings of guilt and remorse
    b. helping them understand their thought disortions and lack of empathy
    c. altering their levels of hormonal stimulation
    d. encouraging them to use denial in minimizing their offenses

12. Eduardo's therapist recommends biofeedback for his high blood pressure because this technique:
    a. helps a person to learn how to regulate autonomic functions.
    b. teaches a person to learn how to regulate peripheral nervous functions.
    c. incorporates structured techniques for managing diet and exercise.
    d. is an effective adjunct to systematic desensitization.

13. The pattern of interrelationships among members of a family is referred to as
    a. family dynamics.
    b. family structure.
    c. interindividual paradigm
    d. psychodynamics.

14. What type of conditioning involves the connection between a neutral stimulus with a naturally evoking stimulus to produce an automatic reflexive response?
    a. instrumental conditioning
    b. aversive conditioning
    c. operant conditioning
    d. classical conditioning

15. _____ is the process through which learning becomes increasingly specific to a given situation.
    a. Generalization
    b. Discrimination
    c. Acquisition
    d. Shaping

16. _____ conditioning is a learning process in which an individual acquires a set of behaviors through reinforcement.
    a. Respondent
    b. Operant
    c. Classical
    d. Pavlovian

17. Which learning technique has been known to parents and animal trainers for many years as a way of establishing complex behaviors through gradual steps?
    a. discrimination training
    b. classical conditioning
    c. punishment
    d. shaping

18. Ideas so deeply entrenched that an individual is not even aware that they lead to disturbing feelings of unhappiness and discouragement are referred to by Beck as
    a. dysfunctional attitudes.
    b. automatic thoughts.
    c. false cognitions.
    d. irrational beliefs.

19. "I must be liked or loved by virtually every other person I come in contact with, otherwise I am worthless." This statement, in Ellis' terms is an example of a(n)
    a. faulty cognition.
    b. dysfunctional attitude.
    c. irrational belief.
    d. activating experience.

20. Two components of systematic desensitization are relaxation training and
    a. positive reinforcement.
    b. construction of a hierarchy of fears.
    c. negative reinforcement.
    d. assertiveness training.

ANSWERS

IDENTIFYING THEORIES

1. FS		6. SL		11. BE	
2. CB		7. BI		12. BI	
3. CB		8. BE		13. CB	
4. BE		9. FS		14. BI	
5. BI		10. BI			

MATCHING

1. f		6. c		11. d	
2. n		7. g		12. a	
3. m		8. b		13. e	
4. i		9. h		14. o	
5. j		10. l		15. k	

SHORT ANSWER

1.
8	Meichenbaum	2	Wolpe	
5	Watson	7	Skinner	
6	Bandura	4	Bateson	
9	Minuchin	3	Pavlov	
1	Ellis			

2.
a.	cognitive restructuring	Forms of behavioral treatment
b.	pituitary gland	Parts of the nervous system
c.	discrimination	Social learning theory terms
d.	Bateson	Social learning theorists
e.	criticism	Forms of positive reinforcement
f.	biofeedback	Genetic concepts

3.

Perspective	Underlying assumption about the causes of psychological disorder	Current evaluation
Family systems	An individual's disorder is a function of disturbance in the family as a whole.	Importance of family increasingly recognized as an influential determinant of some disorders, but rarely are family problems considered the sole basis of serious psychological disturbance.
Behavioral (conditioning models)	Psychological disorder seen as a set of behavioral responses that are controlled by the environment.	These theories are empirically based and straightforward, but lack in-depth approach to understanding the causes of disorders. Cognitive-behavioral models address some of the criticisms of behaviorism but are limited in their application to specific aspects of personality and psychological disorder.
Social learning	Psychological disorder can be acquired through observing the behavior of others.	
Cognitive-behavioral	Dysfunctional emotions are the result of faulty cognitions about the self and others.	
Biological	Psychological disorder has biological origins.	Increasing evidence is accumulating in favor of biological causes of certain disorders, but there is recognition of the importance of interactions with environmental causes.

4.

Theory	Goals of treatment	Approach in therapy
Family systems	To help the client by changing the family system of which the client is a part.	Working with the family as a whole, the therapist attempts to change the dynamics of the family. In some cases, paradoxical interventions may be used.
Behavioral (conditioning models)	Provide corrective learning experiences that reduce the frequency of maladaptive behaviors.	Counterconditioning Systematic desensitization Assertiveness training Contingency management
Social learning	Help client develop more positive self-expectations.	Modeling Self-efficacy training

Theory	Goals of treatment	Approach in therapy
Cognitive-behavioral	Change the dysfunctional thoughts that produce maladaptive emotions.	Cognitive restructuring Rational-emotive therapy Stress inoculation training
Biological	Alter faulty biological processes.	Electroconvulsive therapy Biofeedback

5. The experience of almost falling from a fast-moving roller-coaster.   Fear
   The sight of a roller coaster.   Fear

6.
a. The concordance rate is calculated by determining the ratio of number of relatives who share a disorder divided by the number of relatives who do not share the same disorder.
b. A limitation in the concordance rate is that it does not provide comparison estimates of the effects of genetic inheritance versus contributions of shared family environments.
c. In an adoption study, the contributions of family environment are separated from the contributions of genetic inheritance. When a child who shares the genetic makeup of a parent with a psychological disorder is raised in an environment away from the biological parent, the possible contributing effect of the parent's disorder on the child's development is ruled out.
d. A cross-fostering study makes it possible to study the effects of being raised in an environment by a parent with a psychological disorder when the child has no known genetic predisposition to that disorder.

PSYCH-TAC-TOE

O Gene	O Unconditioned stimulus	X Schedule of reinforcement
O Assertiveness training	X Hippocampus	X Personal constructs
X Paradoxical communication	O Huntington's disease	O Neuron

MULTIPLE CHOICE

1. b	6. b	11. b	16. b
2. a	7. d	12. a	17. d
3. c	8. b	13. a	18. b
4. d	9. b	14. d	19. c
5. a	10 a	15. b	20. b

CHAPTER 6
PERSONALITY DISORDERS

LEARNING OBJECTIVES

1.0 The Nature of Personality Disorders
    1.1 Describe the general features of a personality disorder as diagnosed in DSM-IV.

2.0 Antisocial Personality Disorder
    2.1 Indicate the behaviors that are used to diagnose antisocial personality disorder.
    2.2 Contrast the biological and psychological perspectives on understanding and treating antisocial personality disorder.

3.0 Borderline Personality Disorder
    3.1 Explain the characteristic features of borderline personality disorder.
    3.2 Compare theories and treatment within various perspectives, particularly psychodynamic and cognitive-behavioral.

4.0 Histrionic Personality Disorder
    4.1 Describe the behaviors used to diagnose histrionic personality disorder.
    4.2 Contrast psychodynamic and cognitive-behavioral perspectives on this disorder.

5.0 Narcissistic Personality Disorder
    5.1 Indicate the features used in the diagnosis of narcissistic personality disorder.
    5.2 Compare the approaches favored by psychodynamic and cognitive-behavioral approaches to understanding and treatment.

6.0 Paranoid Personality Disorder
    6.1 Explain the characteristic symptoms of paranoid personality disorder.
    6.2 Differentiate between psychodynamic and cognitive-behavioral explanations of this disorder.

7.0 Schizoid Personality Disorder
    7.1 Describe the features of schizoid personality disorder and its relation to other schizophrenia spectrum disorders.
    7.2 Understand the limitations to treatment of this disorder.

8.0 Schizotypal Personality Disorder
    8.1 Indicate the features used to diagnose schizotypal personality disorder.
    8.2 Describe the relationship between schizophrenia and this personality disorder.

9.0 Avoidant Personality Disorder
    9.1 Explain the diagnostic features of avoidant personality disorder.
    9.2 Compare psychodynamic and cognitive-behavioral approaches to theory and treatment.

10.0 Dependent Personality Disorder
    10.1 Indicate the characteristics of avoidant personality disorder.
    10.2 Differentiate between psychodynamic and cognitive-behavioral approches to this disorder.

11.0 Obsessive-Compulsive Personality Disorder
    11.1 Describe the symptoms of obsessive-compulsive personality disorder.
    11.2 Contrast the psychodynamic and cognitive-behavioral perspectives.

12.0 Chapter Boxes
    12.1 Identify the procedures used in applying brief psychodynamic therapy to people with personality disorders.
    12.2 Explain the differences in prevalence of borderline personality disorder between men and women.
    12.3 Indicate the support for using dimensional models of personality to understand personality disorders.

IDENTIFYING THE DISORDER

Write the name of the personality disorder in the blank next to the symptoms listed.

1. _Antisocial_ — Lack of regard for the legal or moral standards of society, often leading the individual to commit criminal or malicious acts.
2. _Paranoid_ — Unusual suspiciousness of others and constant attempts to guard oneself from harm.
3. _Schizotypal_ — Eccentricities of thought, behavior, appearance, and ways of relating to others, often accompanied by peculiar beliefs.
4. _Borderline_ — Chronic pattern of unstable mood, relationships, and identity.
5. _Dependant_ — Excessive reliance on others, leading the individual to become incapable of making decisions or acting autonomously.
6. _Schizoid_ — Lack of interest in social relationships accompanied by emotional coldness and restrictiveness.
7. _Narcissistic_ — Unrealistic, inflated sense of one's own importance.
8. _Histrionic_ — Overly dramatic emotionality in various realms of everyday behavior.
9. _Avoidant_ — Fearful of closeness to others and terrified by the prospect of being publicly embarrassed.
10. _Obsessive-Compulsive_ — Unusual levels of perfectionism and rigidity.

MATCHING

Put the letter from the right-hand column corresponding to the correct match in the blank next to each item in the left-hand column.

1. _I_ Exaggerated sense of self-importance seen in individuals with narcissistic personality disorder.
2. _F_ Childhood disorder involving criminality that often precedes the development in adulthood of antisocial personality disorder.
3. _H_ Genetic defect once theorized to be a cause of antisocial personality disorder.
4. _K_ Term used to refer to the continuum of disorders including schizophrenia, schizotypal personality disorder, and schizoid personality disorder.
5. ___ Sociologist who proposed that antisocial behavior results from poverty.
6. _N_ Personality trait referring to the extent to which the individual is altruistic, nurturant, and supportive.
7. _BG_ Frequently the goal of treating antisocial personality disorder.
8. ___ Researcher who proposed that people with antisocial personality disorder are relatively insensitive to anxiety-provoking situations.
9. _A_ Personality trait that describes the individual's level of energy, need for stimulation, and interest in relationships with others.
10. ___ Researcher who conducted a landmark long-term study of juvenile delinquents.
11. _E_ Ability to restrain one's immediate urge to act; often lacking in children who later develop antisocial personality disorder.
12. _J_ Term once used for what is now known as schizotypal personality disorder.
13. _B_ Therapeutic approach in which the clinician presents some harsh realities to a client.
14. _O_ Suicidal gesture used to gain attention from others.
15. ___ Cognitive-behavioral theorist who developed a "dialectical" method of therapy for borderline personality disorder.

a. extraversion
b. confrontation
c. Marsha Linehan
d. Lee Robins
e. impulse control
f. latent schizophrenia
g. stimulating feelings of remorse
h. XYY chromosome pattern
i. grandiosity
j. conduct disorder
k. schizophrenia spectrum
l. Robert Merton
m. Hervey Cleckley
n. agreeableness
o. parasuicide

ANSWERS TO CASE THOUGHT QUESTIONS

Try answering each of the thought questions in boxed clinical vignettes in the chapter. Then read the responses provided here for each case and compare them with yours. If your answers are very different from those we have provided, you should then re-read the relevant sections of the text that pertain to the diagnosis exemplified in the case.

Antisocial Personality Disorder (p. 176) Tommy has engaged in brutal acts toward others, drug trafficking, car thefts, counterfeiting, and irresponsibility. Further, he has no regrets for his misdeeds. His lack of remorse suggests that Tommy would be very resistant to participating in treatment. Even if he were forced to enter treatment by a court order, his lack of insight would be a limiting factor in the effectiveness of the treatment.	**Borderline Personality Disorder (p. 180)** Although Lisa shows disturbances in mood, these disturbances are more reflective of personality disorder than mood disorder. She is unpredictable, often becoming uncontrollably angry. The other symptoms of borderline personality disorder are splitting, promiscuity, identity confusion, failure to respect professional boundaries, and a host of self-destructive behaviors. Because of Lisa's disorder, she has troubled relationships with co-workers and supervisors, and engages in inappropriate behavior with clients.
Histrionic Personality Disorder (p. 186) Although Lynette and Lisa have dramatic personal styles, Lynette lacks some of the other symptoms associated with borderline personality disorder such as self-destructiveness, impulsivity, and splitting. It is best not to reinforce histrionic behaviors by becoming overly responsive or sympathetic to "crises." Rather, it is wiser to help people like Lynette develop a clearer perspective what they perceive to be stresses in their lives.	**Narcissistic Personality Disorder (p. 187)** People are put off by Chad's self-absorption, jealousy, and arrogance. It is unlikely that he will succeed in his career because he cannot benefit from constructive criticism or realize where he needs improvement. Even in his mundane job he finds himself in repeated arguments with his supervisor because of his arrogance and grandiosity. Both Lynette and Chad are highly egocentric. Lynette's tendency to create crises causes interpersonal problems, while Chad's annoying interpersonal style alienates other people.
Paranoid Personality Disorder (p. 188) It is very difficult for other people to work with individuals like Anita because they are likely to encounter a deep-rooted suspiciousness that causes them to distance themselves from her. Although Anita's thinking is extreme, she is not delusional. Rather, she is inordinately concerned about the possibility that others might exploit her.	**Schizoid Personality Disorder (p. 189)** It is difficult to know to what extent Pedro's eccentricity is attributable to his personality disorder or to his isolation. Usually, these are interactive processes in which people who remain apart from others act in increasingly strange ways. The diagnosis of schizoid personality disorder is controversial because many people who meet the criteria for this disorder do not feel particularly distressed nor do they harm other people. Nevertheless, this condition is considered a disorder in light of the fact that it is regarded as maladaptive in our society.

Schizotypal Personality Disorder (p. 190)	Avoidant Personality Disorder (p. 191)
Joe avoids other people because of an excessive concern that others might exploit him, whereas Pedro merely prefers to be by himself. Joe's behaviors are regarded as part of the fabric of his personality and they are not so extreme that they would be regarded as being completely out of touch with reality.	Max desperately wishes to be involved with other people while Pedro prefers isolation. In addition, Max is very concerned that he might embarrass himself in front of other people, while Pedro seems oblivious to his impact on others. Because of Max's desire to be closer to other people, there is some potential that he could respond to constructive therapy aimed at changing his behavior and ways of thinking.
Dependent Personality Disorder (p. 192)	Obsessive-compulsive Personality Disorder (p. 193)
Betty's tendency to rely on other people did not originate in her marriage; it was characteristic of her relationships throughout college and probably influenced her choice of a partner. Ken and Betty have developed a system in which Betty is expected to be subservient and dependent, and Ken plays the role of controlling husband.	Trevor's behavior goes beyond ordinary neatness and order in that he has a tyrannical insistence on things being "just right." For example, a fanatical insistence on ordering objects by color and category would be regarded by most people as extreme and pathological. His personal style is so rigid that it stands in the way of his developing close relationships or advancing his career.

SHORT ANSWER

1. Contrast the psychodynamic and cognitive-behavioral explanations of each of the following personality disorders:

Personality disorder	Psychodynamic view	Cognitive-behavioral view
Borderline		
Paranoid		
Histrionic		
Narcissistic		
Avoidant		
Dependent		
Obsessive-compulsive		

2. Summarize the evidence for biological causes of the following personality disorders:

Disorder	Biological explanations
Antisocial personality disorder	
Borderline personality disorder	
Schizoid personality disorder	
Schizotypal personality disorder	

3. Answer the following questions concerning the nature of personality disorders, and their diagnosis and treatment?
a. What is the difference between a personality trait and a personality disorder?
_____
_____

b. What factors do clinicians look for in making diagnoses of personality disorders?
_____
_____

c. What are two major problems involved in diagnosing these disorders?
_____
_____

d. How do clinicians attempt to set goals for treating clients with these disorders?
_____
_____

e. What is the role of a clinician's theoretical perspective in treating people with personality disorders?
_____
_____

4. For each of the following disorders, describe approaches to treatment and problems that are often encountered in implementing these treatments:

Disorder	Approach to treatment	Problems encountered in treatment
Antisocial personality disorder		
Borderline personality disorder		
Paranoid personality disorder		

Disorder	Approach to treatment	Problems encountered in treatment
Schizoid personality disorder		
Dependent personality disorder		
Obsessive-compulsive personality disorder		

MULTIPLE CHOICE

1. Dr. Tobin noted Harold's turbulent relationships, unpredictable emotions, self-destructive behaviors, and identity disturbance and diagnosed him with this personality disorder:
   a. antisocial
   b. paranoid
   c. schizoid
   d. borderline

2. In treating people with antisocial personality disorder, it is recommended that the clinician:
   a. adopt a confrontational approach.
   b. adopt a supportive approach.
   c. supplement psychotherapy with medication.
   d. bring the client's family into treatment.

3. Those who know Lydia have difficulty with her unpredictable vacillation between idealizing and devaluing other people, a symptom known as:
   a. volatility.
   b. splitting.
   c. lability.
   d. ambivalence.

4. Psychodynamic explanations of paranoid personality disorder see it as rooted in the defense mechanism of:
   a. rationalization.
   b. denial.
   c. projection.
   d. reaction formation.

5. Compared to people with avoidant personality disorder, those with schizoid personality disorder:
   a. do not wish to have relationships.
   b. wish to have relationships.
   c. often suffer from a mood disorder.
   d. often are diagnosed with an Axis I disorder.

6. Researchers studying narcissistic and histrionic personality disorders have reported that:
   a. the disorders can be easily differentiated.
   b. features of these two disorders overlap.
   c. both are genetically determined.
   d. they share the feature of hidden paranoia.

7. Cognitive-behavior theorists propose that people with obsessive-compulsive personality disorder:
   a. have a hidden wish to be sloppy and disorderly.
   b. displace sexual energy into obsessional thinking and compulsive behavior.
   c. struggle with seemingly uncontrollable aggressive impulses.
   d. have their self-worth depend on conforming to an ideal abstract of perfectionism.

8. The higher pervalence of borderline personality disorder among women is explained by researchers as due to:
   a. gender bias in the diagnostic criteria.
   b. disturbed family relationships.
   c. biological gender differences.
   d. higher sexual abuse during childhood.

9. A psychologist notes that a client's TAT stories are filled with themes of rage, intense feelings, identity confusion, and fears of abandonment. These themes correspond to which personality disorder?
   a. borderline
   b. antisocial
   c. schizotypal
   d. paranoid

10. When they were children, many adults who are diagnosed with antisocial personality disorder would have met the diagnostic criteria for:
    a. dependent disorder.
    b. conduct disorder.
    c. antisocial disorder.
    d. histrionic disorder.

11. A core feature of people with narcissistic personality disorder is:
    a. depression.
    b. mania.
    c. grandiosity.
    d. splitting.

12. Object relations theorists view people with dependent personality disorder as being:
    a. insecurely attached.
    b. frustrated and hostile.
    c. self-defeating.
    d. passive-aggressive.

13. Diagnosis of a personality disorder is difficult because:
    a. there may be a more specific problem for which the client seeks treatment.
    b. the disorders have such rigid diagnostic criteria.
    c. it is so difficult to detect the disorder in a person's behavior.
    d. these individuals are often aware that they have a problem but avoid seeking treatment.

14. Which brain structure has been linked to aggressive behavior and in particular to antisocial behavior?
    a. hippocampus
    b. hypothalamus
    c. reticular activating system
    d. amygdala

15. A common developmental factor in the psychological environment of individuals with antisocial personality disorder is:
    a. parental drug abuse.
    b. parental disharmony.
    c. abusive siblings.
    d. lack of schooling.

16. An inability to distinguish between one's own identity and the identities of others is characteristic of which personality disorder?
    a. schizoid
    b. self-defeating
    c. borderline
    d. narcissistic

17. In therapy, clients with borderline personality disorder are particularly likely to:
    a. become aloof and distant from the therapist.
    b. describe their problems in vague and ambiguous terms.
    c. become pathologically dependent on the therapist.
    d. show narcissistic behavior.

18. It is difficult to treat people with schizoid and schizotypal personality disorder because:
    a. they are emotionally unstable.
    b. they tend to view their therapist with suspicion.
    c. their treatment is often mandated by the courts.
    d. they are cognitively and emotionally out of touch.

19. According to current psychoanalytic theorists, parental failure to provide reassurance and positive responses to accomplishments may lead to the development of this personality disorder:
    a. histrionic.
    b. schizoid.
    c. schizotypal.
    d. narcissistic.

20. Brief psychodynamic treatment of personality disorders is most likely to be effective when:
    a. the client is resistant to establishing a working relationship.
    b. therapy takes an unfocused and global approach.
    c. there is a prominent interpersonal theme in the client's symptoms.
    d. the therapist avoids confrontation with the client on specific issues.

ANSWERS
IDENTIFYING DISORDERS

1.	Antisocial	6.	Schizoid
2.	Paranoid	7.	Narcissistic
3.	Schizotypal	8.	Histrionic
4.	Borderline	9.	Avoidant
5.	Dependent	10.	Obsessive-compulsive

MATCHING

1.	i	6.	n	11.	e
2.	j	7.	g	12.	f
3.	h	8.	m	13.	b
4.	k	9.	a	14.	o
5.	l	10.	d	15.	c

SHORT ANSWER

1.

Personality disorder	Psychodynamic view	Cognitive-behavioral view
Borderline	Problems in the early development of the self due to parents who either do not allow the child to achieve an independent identity or who are physically, emotionally or sexually abusive.	Dichotomous thinking about the self and others and low sense of self-efficacy leading to lack of confidence, low motivation, and inability to seek long-term goals.
Paranoid	Heavy reliance on the defense mechanism of projection.	Mistaken assumptions that people will harm you if they get the chance, and that one needs to be wary of the malicious motives of others.
Histrionic	Traditional view is that histrionic personality disorder is a variant of hysteria, the product of unresolved Oedipal conflicts and over-reliance on the defense mechanism of repression. Other psycho-analytic theorists propose that the disorder is the result of a global cognitive style that cannot focus on details in life situations.	Mistaken assumption is that one is unable to handle life on one's own, causing the individual to seek someone else to make up for this deficit. The global nature of the individual's cognitive style leads to diffuse and exaggerated emotional states and unstable evaluations of others.
Narcissistic	Traditional explanation is that the disorder is due to failure to progress beyond early psychosexual stages of development. Object relations theorists propose that the individual develops the disorder in response to faulty parenting, in which the child is made to feel insecure and inadequate. This type of parenting leads the child to develop a false grandiose view of the self.	Faulty belief that one is special and deserves to be treated better than other people. Problems result when these grandiose ideas about the self clash with experiences in the real world.
Avoidant	Horney's theory proposes that avoidant personality represents a "turning away from others" due to expectation that one will be criticized and rejected.	Hypersensitivity to rejection occurs due to childhood experiences of extreme criticism by parents. This leads to the faulty belief that one is flawed and unworthy and undeserving of the attention and friendship of others. Avoidance develops as a means of protection from this anticipated rejection.
Dependent	Traditional view is that the disorder reflects regression to or fixation at the oral stage of development due to overindulgence or neglect by parents of dependency needs. Object relations theorists view the disorder as the result of insecure attachment and low self-esteem.	Unassertiveness and anxiety over making independent decisions result from doubts about one's adequacy and ability to solve problems. Assertiveness with others would threaten the security of relationships.
Obsessive-compulsive	Traditional view is that the disorder is due to fixation at or regression to the anal stage of psychosexual development. More recent views emphasize an overly narrow and rigid cognitive style.	Unrealistic concern about being perfect and avoiding mistakes.

2.

Disorder	Biological explanations
Antisocial personality disorder	Extra chromosome (XYY pattern) Excess of testosterone Defects in frontal lobes of cortex and/or limbic system Neuropsychological deficits in learning and attention Genetic inheritance
Borderline personality disorder	Genetic inheritance Abnormal neuroendocrine functions Electrophysiological functions
Schizoid personality disorder	Genetic inheritance, possibly linked to schizophrenia
Schizotypal personality disorder	Genetic inheritance, possibly reflecting a latent form of schizophrenia

3.

a. A personality trait is an enduring pattern as is a personality disorder, but a personality disorder is specifically identified as creating difficulties in the individual's life or feelings of personal distress.
b. The clinician looks at the client's overall life history to determine whether the current problems have been present on a long-standing basis.
c. The client often seeks treatment for other problems such as depression.
    Many personality disorders share similar features.
d. Rather than seek complete personality change, clinicians tend to focus their work on achieving a set of more limited, but realizable goals that will help alleviate the client's current distress.
e. Most clinicians tend to individualize their treatment for the client's particular disorder and integrate relevant theoretical perspectives that are most appropriate for the client's disorder.

4.

Disorder	Approach to treatment	Problems encountered in treatment
Antisocial personality disorder	Stimulate realization that client's behavior has caused harm to others. Reflect the selfish and self-defeating nature of the client's behavior.	Individuals with this disorder often do not seek help voluntarily and when in treatment, do not change easily.
Borderline personality disorder	Combine an approach that uses confrontation of client's maladaptive thoughts and defenses with providing a sense of stability and predictability. Help client recognize self-destructive nature of certain high-risk or harmful behaviors. Medication may also be used to alleviate symptoms of depression and anxiety.	Their volatility, inconsistency, and intensity make it difficult for these clients to remain in therapy. At the same time, clients may become pathologically dependent on their therapists.

Disorder	Approach to treatment	Problems encountered in treatment
Paranoid personality disorder	Cognitive-behavioral approach suggests countering client's mistaken assumptions and increasing client's self-efficacy. Generally, it is important to collaborate with the client, increase the client's awareness of other points of view, and help client become more assertive.	Client is likely to be distrustful of therapist and the therapy process.
Schizoid personality disorders	Help client clarify communication skills and modify isolated and eccentric behaviors.	Clients tend to be cognitively and emotionally inaccessible. Progress is likely to be slow and limited in scope.
Obsessive-compulsive personality disorder	Focusing on client's maladaptive thoughts, possibly combining this approach with paradoxical instructions to become more symptomatic.	Obsessive-compulsive client tends to ruminate excessively, and therapy might feed into this process.

MULTIPLE CHOICE

1. d	6. b	11. c	16. c
2. a	7. d	12. a	17. c
3. b	8. d	13. a	18. d
4. c	9. a	14. d	19. d
5. a	10. b	15. b	20. c

CHAPTER 7
ANXIETY DISORDERS

LEARNING OBJECTIVES

1.0 The Nature of Anxiety Disorders
    1.1 Describe the characteristics of anxiety symptoms.
    1.2 Differentiate between fear and anxiety.
2.0 Panic Disorder
    2.1 Explain the characteristic features of panic disorder and the symptoms of the related disorder, agoraphobia.
    2.2 Contrast biological, behavioral, and cognitive-behavioral approaches to understanding and treating panic disorder.
3.0 Specific Phobias
    3.1 Indicate the features used to diagnose specific phobias.
    3.2 Discuss the cognitive-behavioral, behavioral, and biological perspectives on theory and treatment.
4.0 Social Phobia
    4.1 Describe the symptoms of people with social phobia.
    4.2 Explain how social phobia develops and how behavioral and cognitive-behavioral methods can be used in treatment.
5.0 Generalized Anxiety Disorder
    5.1 Indicate the symptoms used in the diagnosis of generalized anxiety disorder.
    5.2 Describe how biological and life stress approaches can contribute to understanding and treatment.
6.0 Obsessive-Compulsive Disorder
    6.1 Enumerate the diagnostic criteria of obsessive-compulsive disorder.
    6.2 Compare behavioral, cognitive-behavioral, and biological perspectives.
7.0 Acute Stress Disorder and Post-Traumatic Stress Disorder
    7.1 Describe the features of acute stress disorder and post-traumatic stress disorder.
    7.2 Discuss the relationship between severity of symptoms and exposure to stressors.
    7.3 Indicate the issues involved in understanding the role of trauma in psychological disorders, and approaches to treatment that involve biological, behavioral, and cognitive-behavioral methods.
8.0 Chapter Boxes
    8.1 Explain the controversy regarding psychosurgery for extreme treatment-resistant cases of obsessive-compulsive disorder.
    8.2 Describe research concerning the long-term effects of psychological trauma.
    8.3 Indicate the age variations of anxiety over the life span.

IDENTIFYING DISORDERS

Put the name of the anxiety disorder in the blank next to the symptom using the following abbreviations:

PD= Panic disorder   **SpP**= Specific phobia
SoP= Social phobia   **OCD**= Obsessive-compulsive disorder
GAD= Generalized anxiety disorder   **PTSD**= Post-traumatic stress disorder

Disorder	**Symptom**		**Disorder**	**Symptom**
1. ____	Flashbacks.		5. ____	Repetitive thoughts and behaviors that cannot be controlled.
2. ____	Inability to perform tasks in public.			
3. ____	Excessive worrying about minor problems.		6. ____	Fear of particular objects, activities, or situations.
4. ____	Intense fear accompanied by loss of control.			

Disorder	Symptom		Disorder	Symptom
7. ___	Avoidance of places where one might be trapped and have an anxiety attack.		10. ___	Avoidance of feared objects, activities, or situations.
8. ___	Chronic sense of edginess, worry, dread, and irritability.		11. ___	Fear of public embarrassment or humiliation.
9. ___	Time-consuming, unnecessary rituals that cannot be controlled.		12. ___	Denial of an unpleasant, disastrous event.

MATCHING

Put the letter from the right-hand column corresponding to the correct match in the blank next to each item in the left-hand column.

1. ___ Behavioral treatment in which the client is trained to substitute a new response to anxiety in the presence of a feared stimulus.
2. ___ Anxiety disorder involving extreme fear of public humiliation.
3. ___ Type of panic attack that arises without a situational cue.
4. ___ Heightened sensitivity to stimuli in the environment.
5. ___ Most effective medication for treating anxiety symptoms.
6. ___ Type of panic attack that does not occur with every exposure in every instance of exposure to a possible threat.
7. ___ Learned associations between internal or external cues and feelings of anxiety.
8. ___ Fear of being trapped or stranded without help.
9. ___ Type of panic attack that occurs with each exposure to a stimulus or cue.
10. ___ Behavioral treatment involving reduction of muscular tension.
11. ___ Medication used in treating obsessive compulsive disorder.
12. ___ Cognitive-behavioral treatment of anxiety disorders in which client learns to discontinue anxiety-related ideas.
13. ___ Anxiety disorder involving repetitive uncontrollable thoughts and behaviors.
14. ___ Explanation of panic disorder with agoraphobia based on cognitive-behavioral theory.
15. ___ Behavioral treatment in which the therapist subjects the client to feared stimuli until anxiety diminishes.

a.   conditioned fear reactions
b.   situationally predisposed
c.   agoraphobia
d.   counterconditioning
e.   situationally bound
f.   social phobia
g.   flooding
h.   hypervigilance
i.   unexpected
j.   clomipramine
k.   relaxation training
l.   obsessive-compulsive disorder
m.   fear of fear
n.   thought stopping
o.   benzodiazepines

ANSWERS TO CASE THOUGHT QUESTIONS

Try answering each of the thought questions in boxed clinical vignettes in the chapter. Then read the responses provided here for each case and compare them with yours. If your answers are very different from those we have provided, you should then re-read the relevant sections of the text that pertain to the diagnosis exemplified in the case.

Panic Disorder without Agoraphobia (p. 207)	**Specific Phobia (p. 212)**
Frieda has agoraphobia as indicated by her reluctance to leave her house due to fear of having an attack.	The symptoms shown by Herbert include irrational fear, avoidance of the feared situation, extreme measures taken to ensure his safety, and interference with his social responsibilities.
The panic attacks led Frieda to fear being outside the home where she could not obtain help were she to have an attack.	Herbert's symptoms are not indicative of agoraphobia as his reluctance to leave the house is not due to fear of being stranded or trapped without help.

Social Phobia (p. 215)	Generalized Anxiety Disorder (p. 217)
Ted shows physical and psychological symptoms of anxiety when confronted with the feared situation of public speaking. Because he avoids speaking in public, Ted does not have the opportunity to bolster his sense of self-efficacy.	In addition to Gina's concerns about parenting and financial pressures, she has several symptoms including a chronic sense of discomfort and tension, and experiences of physical symptoms that have no physiological basis. Unlike a person suffering from panic disorder who has episodes of anxiety, Gina's experience of anxiety is more continuous and unconnected with events in her life.
Obsessive-Compulsive Disorder (p. 220)	**Post-Traumatic Stress Disorder (p. 224)**
Mark's obsession is the thought that the outlet will cause harm; his compulsion is his behavior of shining the flashlight into the outlet whenever he enters or leaves the classroom. The personality disorder involves inflexibility in thinking and behavior; obsessive-compulsive disorder involves intrusive thoughts that can be alleviated only by engaging in patterns of rigid, ritualistic behaviors.	Steve's feelings of guilt are so severe that he would probably not be reassured by simply being told that he did all he could to help his friends. In light of the fact that disturbing experiences preceded his alcohol use, it is likely that stress rather than alcohol is the cause. It is possible that alcohol exacerbates Steve's flashbacks and nightmares.

SHORT ANSWER

1. Describe the role of the following neurotransmitters in anxiety disorders:

Neurotransmitter	Role in anxiety disorders
Serotonin	
GABA	
Norepinephrine	

2. A behavior therapist is working with a client who has a spider phobia. Describe what treatment approach would be involved in each of the following methods:

Method	Treatment approach
Systematic desensitization	
Graded *in vivo* exposure	
Imaginal flooding	
Flooded *in vivo* exposure	

3. For each of the three approaches used in treating obsessive-compulsive disorder, indicate the mechanism of action and specify a limitation or disadvantage of each approach:

Method	Mechanism of action	Limitation or problem
Behavioral		
Medications		
Psychosurgery		

4. Answer the following questions regarding the long-term effects of psychological trauma:

a. As discussed in the Research Focus, what are six possible long-term effects on women of sexual or physical abuse?

_____   _____
_____   _____
_____   _____

b. What eight factors are likely to increase the chances that a person exposed to trauma will suffer symptoms of PTSD?

_____   _____
_____   _____
_____   _____
_____   _____

c. List five types of treatments that are used for PTSD:

_____   _____
_____   _____
_____

5. Summarize three forms of evidence used to support the role of biology in obsessive-compulsive disorder:

_____
_____
_____

6. Indicate the main differences between social phobia and panic disorder with agoraphobia:

Social phobia	Panic disorder with agoraphobia

7. Summarize the cognitive-behavioral perspective as applied to each of the following anxiety disorders:

Disorder	Cognitive-behavioral explanation
Panic disorder with agoraphobia	
Specific phobia	
Social phobia	
Generalized anxiety disorder	
Post-traumatic stress disorder	

ACROSTIC

Fill in the boxes in the items on the left and place the letter with the number below it in the same numbered space at top of puzzle; when the puzzle is correctly solved, you will have the name of a condition related to anxiety disorders.

1 2 3 4 5 6 7 8 9 10 11

Period of intense fear accompanied by feeling a loss of control.
6

Medication most effective in treating symptoms of anxiety.
9

Extreme somatic treatment used to treat obsessive-compulsive disorder.
2

Systematic desensitization and flooding are behavioral methods that involve _____ to the threatening situation.
4

Phase in PTSD in which flashbacks occur.
8

Phobia characterized by anxiety over public performance.
1

According to one theory, panic attacks are caused by an excess of this chemical in the blood.
5

Live presentation of a feared stimulus is used in this form of behavior therapy.
10

_____ stopping is used in this form of behavioral therapy.
7

The trade name of fluoxetine, a medication that alters serotonin levels in the brain.
3

A _____ event is a life-threatening event that has severe psychological and physiological effects.
11

MULTIPLE CHOICE

1. Which anxiety disorder is most common in young children?
   a. separation anxiety disorder
   b. obsessive compulsive disorder
   c. generalized anxiety disorder
   d. panic disorder with agoraphobia

2. In people with panic disorder, the association of uncomfortable bodily sensations with memories of the last panic attack can lead to a full-blown panic attack, a phenomenon known as:
   a. unconditioned response.
   b. anticipatory response.
   c. conditioned fear reaction.
   d. pre-panic aura.

3. Henri's job involves taking an elevator to the 35th floor but his claustrophobia is creating serious problems. His therapist describes vivid descriptions of people trapped in elevators, and asks Henri to imagine the scenes, an approach called:
   a. imaginal flooding.
   b. systematic desensitization.
   c. in vivo desensitization.
   d. decompensation.

4. Edward's therapist recommended this antidepressant medication for his obsessive-compulsive disorder:
   a. chlorpromazine
   b. chlorazepam
   c. clozapine
   d. clomipramine

5. Following a traumatic life event, people go through a series of characteristic responses. The initial reaction, involving a sense of alarm and strong emotion, is called the:
   a. outcry phase.
   b. denial/intrusion phase.
   c. traumatic phase.
   d. intrusion phase.

6. The surgical treatment used in extreme cases of obsessive-compulsive disorder is known as:
   a. cingulotomy.
   b. hyperthyroidism.
   c. uncovering.
   d. lactate infusion.

7. Treatment of Barbara Wilder began in her home in which she was guided step-by-step through situations that approximated those situations that had terrified her in the past, techniques known as:
   a. flooding and medication.
   b. hypnosis and age regression.
   c. symptom mastery and cognitive structuring.
   d. in vivo techniques and graded exposure.

8. Marlene told her therapist that since her rape she has been terrorized by experiences that seem like hallucinations, similar to those that she once had following LSD use. These experiences are called:
   a. flashbacks.
   b. intrusions.
   c. delusions.
   d. obsessions.

9. Which neurotransmitter is activated when an individual is placed under stress or in a dangerous situation?
   a. GABA
   b norepinephrine
   c. serotonin
   d. acetylcholine

10. Every time that Jonathan sees a spider, he experiences extreme fear and anxiety. Jonathan would be diagnosed as having:
    a. generalized anxiety disorder.
    b. aversion disorder.
    c. obsessive-compulsive disorder.
    d. specific phobia.

11. A woman feels that she must scrub her hands for exactly ten minutes after eating any food. This behavior is called:
    a. an obsession.
    b. a compulsion.
    c. a delusion.
    d. a specific phobia.

12. This type of panic attack is an essential element of the diagnosis of panic disorder:
    a. situationally bound
    b. situationally predisposed
    c. agoraphobic
    d. unexpected (uncued)

13. To which chemical in the blood do individuals with panic disorder seem hypersensitive?
    a. insulin
    b. norepinephrine
    c. progesterone
    d. lactate

14. The most effective antianxiety medications are called:
    a. neuroleptics.
    b. amphetamines.
    c. benzodiazepines.
    d. narcotics.

15. Which behavioral technique is often successful in the treatment of panic disorder with agoraphobia?
    a. lactate therapy
    b. modeling
    c. relaxation training
    d. flooding

16. Which theoretical perspective views the causes of phobias to be based on the individual's faulty inferences and generalizations?
    a. cognitive
    b. humanistic
    c. existential
    d. psychoanalytic

17. The cognitive-behavioral method in which the client is taught not to have anxiety provoking thoughts is called:
    a. imaginal flooding.
    b. thought stopping.
    c. graded thinking.
    d. *in vivo* desensitization.

18. A cognitive-behavioral therapist would treat an individual with generalized anxiety disorder by:
    a. teaching the client to recognize and change anxiety-producing thoughts.
    b. using free association to illuminate unconscious conflicts.
    c. actively and empathically listening to the client's concerns.
    d. urging the client to develop an enhanced sense of self .

19. Panic disorder in women is associated with this early childhood experience:
    a. parental illness and substance abuse
    b. overachieving school performance
    c. overindulgence by parental figures
    d. supportive family environment

20. In the treatment of PTSD, clinicians may administer medication to control:
    a. impulsivity.
    b. appetite disturbance.
    c. high level of sociability.
    d. anxiety, depression, or nightmares.

ANSWERS
IDENTIFYING DISORDERS

1. PTSD	5. OCD	9. OCD
2. SoP	6. SpP	10. SpP
3. GAD	7. PD	11. SoP
4. PD	8. GAD	12. PTSD

MATCHING

1. d	6. b	11. j
2. f	7. a	12. n
3. i	8. c	13. l
4. h	9. e	14. m
5. o	10. k	15. g

SHORT ANSWER
1.

Neurotransmitter	Role in anxiety disorders
Serotonin	Deficiency of serotonin may be involved in panic disorders, as indicated by efficacy of treatment by fluoxetine, which increases availability of serotonin in the brain.
GABA	It is proposed that panic disorder is due to GABA deficiency; neurons in subcortical brain areas involved in panic attacks become more active with less GABA to inhibit them.
Norepinephrine	There is some evidence that panic disorder is caused by heightened levels of norepinephrine when the individual is placed under stress.

2.

Method	Treatment approach
Systematic desensitization	Teaching the client to relax while imagining coming closer and closer to touching a spider.
Graded *in vivo* exposure	Exposing the client in steps to an actual spider.
Imaginal flooding	Instructing the client to imagine touching and holding a spider.
Flooded *in vivo* exposure	Giving the client a spider to touch and hold until the client no longer feels anxiety.

3.

Method	Mechanism of action	Limitation or problem
Behavioral	Thought-stopping to reduce obsessional thinking; exposure to situations that provoke the compulsions or obsessions.	Is successful in 75% of cases but does not reduce symptoms in the remaining 25% who enter treatment.
Medications	May compensate for serotonin deficiencies in certain individuals with the disorder.	Not effective for all individuals with the disorder.
Psychosur-gery	Cutting neuronal tracts between the frontal lobe and a part of the limbic system.	A radical intervention reserved only for clients who are resistant to other treatment methods.

4. a.
depression
anxiety
substance abuse
sexual dysfunction
dissociation
interpersonal problems

b.
dissociative symptoms
loss of autonomy
stressful life experiences
greater extent of trauma
prior psychological symptoms
demographic factors
childhood exposure to trauma
genetic predisposition

c.
pharmacological
conditioning
improved coping
"covering" techniques
"uncovering" techniques

5.
There is a higher concordance rate in monozygotic compared to dizygotic twins.
Symptoms of obsessive-compulsive disorder have been observed in people with neurological disorders that affect the basal ganglia. Brain imaging studies suggest that there is increased metabolic activity in the basal ganglia and frontal lobes.

6.

Social phobia	Panic disorder with agoraphobia
Anxiety is specific to potentially embarrassing contexts in which one's behavior might be observed by others.	The individual fears going out of a safe place due to a concern that a panic attack may strike.
No unusual response to lactate injection.	Lactate injection can provoke the experience of a panic attack.
Equally common in men and women	More common in women than men.

7.

Disorder	Cognitive-behavioral explanation
Panic disorder with agoraphobia	Fear of fear.
Specific phobia	Faulty inferences and overgeneralizations.
Social phobia	Focus attention on imagined criticism.
Generalized anxiety disorder	Focus on worries which leads to a vicious cycle.
Post-traumatic stress disorder	Excessive guilt and self-blame for traumatic events.

ACROSTIC

PANIC ATTACK	LACTATE
BENZODIAZEPINES	IN VIVO
PSYCHOSURGERY	THOUGHT
EXPOSURE	PROZAC
INTRUSION	TRAUMATIC
SOCIAL	

MULTIPLE CHOICE

1.	a	11.	b	
2.	c	12.	d	
3.	a	13.	d	
4.	d	14.	c	
5.	a	15.	c	
6.	a	16.	a	
7.	d	17.	b	
8.	a	18.	a	
9.	b	19.	a	
10.	d	20.	d	

CHAPTER 8
SOMATOFORM DISORDERS, PSYCHOPHYSIOLOGICAL CONDITIONS, AND DISSOCIATIVE DISORDERS

LEARNING OBJECTIVES

1.0 Somatoform Disorders
    1.1 Describe somatoform disorders as the translation of psychological conflicts into physical symptoms.
    1.2 Indicate the symptoms of conversion disorder.
    1.3 Enumerate the diagnostic features of somatization disorder.
    1.4 Describe the characteristics of body dysmorphic disorder.
    1.5 Indicate the symptoms used to diagnose hypochondriasis.
    1.6 Contrast the psychodynamic and behavioral approaches to somatoform disorders.
2.0 Psychophysiological Conditions
    2.1 Explain the basis of the DSM-IV category of psychological factors affecting physical condition, including psychophysiological disorders and sleep disorders.
    2.2 Discuss approaches to understanding and treating stress-related disorders, including life events models, models of coping, psychoneuroimmunology, personality traits, and behavioral medicine.
3.0 Dissociative Disorders
    3.1 Indicate the symptoms used in the diagnosis of dissociative identity disorder, explanations of this disorder as due to trauma, and the use of hypnotherapy and cognitive-behavioral treatment methods.
    3.2 Describe the symptoms of dissociative amnesia.
    3.3 Enumerate the diagnostic criteria for dissociative fugue.
    3.4 Indicate the symptoms used to diagnose depersonalization disorder.
    3.5 Discuss the role of trauma as a cause of dissociative disorders.
4.0 Chapter Boxes
    4.1 Discuss the difficulty involved in distinguishing a medical illness from a somatoform disorder.
    4.2 Explain the evidence for increased risk of hypertension among African-Americans.
    4.3 Indicate the nature of the research evidence supporting dissociative identity disorder as a legal defense.

IDENTIFYING DISORDERS

Write the name of the disorder in the blank next to the symptoms listed.
1. _____ Misinterpretation of normal bodily signs as indicators of disease.
2. _____ State of confusion about personal identity accompanied by a flight from home.
3. _____ Translation of psychological conflict into a set of specific physical symptoms.
4. _____ Disturbance in sleep and daytime functioning due to disrupted sleep-wake schedule.
5. _____ Complaints of physical pain that have no physiological basis.
6. _____ Exaggerated and unrealistic dissatisfaction with a part of one's body.
7. _____ Continued experiences of waking up suddenly and in a panic from sound sleep.
8. _____ Development of more than one self within the same individual.
9. _____ Chronic form of factitious disorder in which person's life becomes consumed with pursuit of medical care.
10. _____ Chronic difficulty with getting to sleep.
11. _____ Psychological issues expressed through multiple and recurrent physical symptoms.
12. _____ Recurrent and persistent episodes of feeling disconnected from one's own body.

13. _____ Continuous feeling of a need for sleep and of never being fully rested.
14. _____ Deliberate fabrication of physical or psychological symptoms for an ulterior motive.
15. _____ Inability to remember personal details and experiences not due to brain damage.
16. _____ Feigning of symptoms due to inner need to maintain a sick role.

MATCHING

Put the letter from the right-hand column corresponding to the correct match in the blank next to each item in the left-hand column.

1. ___ Field that focuses on study of connections among stress, the nervous system, and the immune system.
2. ___ Treatment shown to be effective for dissociative identity disorder.
3. ___ Condition in which individual feigns signs of physical illness for an ulterior motive.
4. ___ Condition in which normal bodily signs are interpreted as symptoms of disease.
5. ___ A fully developed personality in dissociative identity disorder that is separate from the main personality.
6. ___ Disorders in which a person's physical problems are temporally linked to a stressful event.
7. ___ Disorder in which person induces symptoms in another who is under the individual's care.
8. ___ The primary personality in multiple personality disorder.
9. ___ A method of coping in which a person reduces stress by trying to feel better about the situation.
10. ___ Personality type characterized by impatience, irritability, competitiveness, and time pressure.
11. ___ Interdisciplinary approach to psychophysiological disorders in which clients are taught to gain control over physical problems.
12. ___ Coping style that involves taking action to address the situation.
13. ___ Inability to remember events occuring in a specific time period.
14. ___ Personality type characterized by suppressed emotions, compliance, and conformity.
15. ___ Condition in which a person feeling distressed and unhappy seeks therapy for a physical disorder.

a. psychoneuroimmunology
b. behavioral medicine
c. localized amnesia
d. host
e. masked depression
f. Type C personality
g. malingering
h. hypnotherapy
i. alter
j. emotion-focused coping
k. Type A personality
l. psychophysiological
m. factitious disorder by proxy
n hypochondriasis
o. problem-focused coping

ANSWERS TO CASE THOUGHT QUESTIONS

Try answering each of the thought questions in boxed clinical vignettes in the chapter. Then read the responses provided here for each case and compare them with yours. If your answers are very different from those we have provided, you should then re-read the relevant sections of the text that pertain to the diagnosis exemplified in the case.

Conversion Disorder (p. 240)	**Somatization Disorder (p. 241)**
Tiffany has recently been under stress and she seems to be somewhat prone to overreacting to situations. The accident in which Tiffany was involved was caused by her "not seeing" the elderly man on the side of the road. Her subsequent loss of vision may be seen as related to unconscious feelings of guilt over her action.	Helen's symptoms include memory loss, blurry vision, fatigue, difficulty swallowing, nausea, loss of sexual interest, painful menstruation, vague gynecological complaints, and aching legs. Her physician believes that these have no medical basis. Helen may feel unfulfilled and constrained in her role as homemaker as well as loss of intimacy with her husband.

Pain Disorder (p. 242)	Body Dysmorphic Disorder (p. 243)
Brian's physical complaints are limited to pain which apparently has no physical basis. Although corroborating evidence would be necessary, it might appear that Brian is seeking to take a break from the pressures of his career. It is more likely that Brian's symptoms are not deliberately faked, however, but that they might reflect underlying conflict regarding the demands of his job.	Lydia has an exaggerated concern about the size of her hands that does not coincide with medical opinion or the opinions of those who know her. In answering this question, consider whether Lydia's concern with her hands might reflect a deeper discontent with herself that would not be alleviated by surgery.
Hypochondriasis (p. 244)	**Malingering (p. 246)**
It is possible that Beth's concern with her symptoms is the reflection of distress about her children moving away from home. If Beth's symptoms persist, it is more likely that her hypochondriasis is not transient. Beth has actually experienced irregular and heavy menstrual periods. These physical symptoms have a physiological basis (she probably is going through menopause) and are therefore different from those of a person with somatization or conversion disorder whose physical complaints do not have a physiological basis.	Although Linda actually experienced a fall that caused her to bruise her knee, her reaction seems exaggerated (as verified by medical assessments). Further, Linda claims that the accident occurred at an unfortunate time in her life, but it is more likely that she would benefit from being able to stay home from work and support her young daughter through disability payments. Unlike Helen, Linda has one major physical complaint. Further, unlike Helen, Linda would derive benefit from being diagnosed as having a medical problem that resulted from her fall.
Psychophysiological Condition (p. 247)	**Dissociative Identity Disorder (p. 258)**
Brenda has had a long history of emotional problems. She seems to be aware of the fact that her inner tension dates back to her troubled relationship with her parents. She has experienced this tension in the form of somatic symptoms including headaches and stomachaches. Presumably Brenda's headaches and stomachaches are genuine physical reactions that can be medically diagnosed. By contrast, the symptoms of a somatoform disorder usually lack an understandable medical basis.	Myra's therapist would look for evidence of past abuse or other trauma in her early life. The host personality is reserved, traditional, and conservative; her alters express constrasting traits and lifestyles.
Dissociative Amnesia (p. 260)	**Dissociative Fugue (p. 260)**
A clinician would need to conduct physical and neuropsychological assessments to determine if her amnesia is caused by brain damage. Norma experienced a severe trauma when she saw her daughter hit by a car, and the stress from this incident may have triggered the amnestic episode.	Without warning, George left his home and job, moved to a new city, and forgot his previous identity. It is possible that George was deeply troubled by the impending loss of his job due to the closing of the college.

Depersonalization Disorder (p. 261)
Robert's therapist would try to determine whether or not Robert was aware of his experiences as being abnormal. People with hallucinations believe that their perceptions are real.

Although Robert describes his episodes of depersonalization as "nervous attacks," there is no evidence that he is in fact overwhelmed with anxiety nor the feeling of loss of control.

ANAGRAMS

Rearrange the letters for each item so that they form a word which fits the definition. When you have completed each item, arrange the large bold letters so that they form another term.

1. **I** N V E C **N** R S O   A somatoform disorder in which unacceptable drives or conflicts are translated into physical symptoms.

2. R **A** P R Y M I   A kind of gain involving relief from anxiety or responsibility due to the development of physical or psychological symptoms.

3. S P O S I **H N** Y   Technique used in therapy for dissociative identity disorder.

4. G **U** F **E** U   Condition in which an individual becomes confused about personal identity and travels unexpectedly away from home.

5. S O P H M I R **C** D Y   In body _____ disorder, the individual is intensely dissatisfied with a part of his or her own body.

6. **M** U A R T A   Type of experience commonly in the backgrounds of people with dissociative identity disorder.

Syndrome in which the individual's life becomes consumed with the pursuit of medical care:

_ _ _ _ _ _ _ _ _ _ ' _

SHORT ANSWER

1. List five reasons for the misdiagnosis of dissociative identity disorder:

_____   _____

_____   _____

_____

2. Explain how each of the following contributes to the way an individual responds to stressful situations:

Context	
Internal or personal qualities	
External or situational resources	

3. Specify the type of amnesia that applies to each of the following cases (assume the amnesia applied only to the period or memory loss described):

	A man forgets everything that happened during the month while his wife was dying of cancer.
	A young woman has no recall of events in her past life following her duty in the Persian Gulf war.
	A man forgets the type of car he drove before a hurricane hit his community.
	An incest victim remembers her childhood only through the time when she was abused.

4. Place an "X" next to the term or name that does not belong with the others:

a. Motor disturbances
Localized amnesia
Sensory disturbances
Symptoms simulating physical illness

b. Malingering
Factitious disorder
Hypochondriasis
Munchausen syndrome

c. Dissociative identity disorder
Pain disorder
Depersonalization disorder
Dissociative amnesia

d. Briquet   e. Primary gain
  Charcot   Trauma
  Janet   Secondary gain
  Kluft   Unconscious guilt

5. Contrast the relationship between psychological and physical aspects of functioning represented in each of the following disorders:

Disorder	Nature of physical complaint	Presence of actual physical symptoms	Theorized role of psychological factors
Conversion disorder			
Somatization disorder			
Somatoform pain disorder			
Body dysmorphic disorder			
Hypochondriasis			
Factitious disorder			
Psychophysio-logical conditions			

6. Answer the following questions regarding the relationship between psychological factors and physical health:

a. What is the relationship between the terms "psychological factors affecting physical condition" and "psychosomatic illness"?

_____

_____

b. What is the relationship between the terms "psychological factors affecting physical condition" and "psychophysiological disorders"?

_____

_____

c. How is stress thought to lead to the development of physical symptoms?

_____

_____

d. What does research indicate about the effects of emotional expression on a person's ability to recover from stress?

_____

_____

e. What is the explanation of the relationship between the Type C personality and cancer?

_____

_____

f. How is Type A personality thought to be related to heart disease?

_____

_____

7. Describe one positive aspect and one negative aspect of primary and secondary gain from the point of view of the individual with a somatoform disorder:

Type of gain	Positive aspect	Negative aspect
Primary		
Secondary		

8. Describe one problem involved in the treatment of somatoform disorder, dissociative identity disorder, and other dissociative disorders:

Disorder	Problem involved in treatment
Somatoform disorder	
Dissociative identity disorder	
Other dissociative disorders	

9. A woman has just been told that her daughter is in trouble at school, an event that she perceives as stressful. Contrast the emotion-focused and problem-focused ways of coping with this stress in terms of the categories below:

Coping method	Example	Possible positive outcome	Possible negative outcome
Emotion-focused			
Problem-focused			

10.

a. Sam exercises for half an hour before he goes to bed, because it is the only chance he has. He drinks coffee continuously throughout the day, with his last cup after dinner. Since his room is fairly small, he does all his studying on his bed. His unpredictable work hours lead Sam to sleep at different times on different days. Lately, Sam has been feeling exhausted and that he has not been able to sleep enough, and is very worried about this. What are Sam's bad sleep habits?

_____

_____

_____

_____

_____

b. What psychological treatments might a clinician recommend for Sam to improve his sleep?

_____

_____

_____

MULTIPLE CHOICE

1. Rose Marston had no motive for feigning illness and truly believed she had a physical disorder. These factors led to the diagnosis of:
   a. factitious disorder.
   b. malingering.
   c. somatization disorder.
   d. body dysmorphic diso

rder.

2. Job stress often causes Ralph's ulcer to flare up. Ralph seems to have a:
   a. psychophysiological condition.
   b. somatoform disorder.
   c. factitious disorder.
   d. dissociative disorder.

3. The behavior characterized by being hard-driving, competitive, and impatient, associated with heart disease is called Type:
   a. Z pattern.
   b. B pattern.
   c. C pattern.
   d. A pattern.

4. Researchers urge caution before diagnosing a conversion disorder, because as many as half of those diagnosed as having conversion disorder turn out years later to have had:
   a. a true physical illness.
   b. a true psychological disorder.
   c. hypochrondriacal symptoms.
   d. dissociative symptoms.

5. People with somatization rarely seek out psychotherapy volunatrily because they:
   a. lack the financial resources to pay for therapy.
   b. fear that the clinician might detect their motive for feigning illness.
   c. do not consider their physical difficulties to have an emotional cause.
   d. are too embarrassed to talk about their physical problems.

6. Each of the following disorders involves unexplainable medical symptoms except:
   a. hypochondriasis.
   b. somatization disorder.
   c. somatoform pain disorder.
   d. conversion disorder.

7. Marlene has repeatedly tried to make her 11-month-old son physically ill, so that she can rush him to the emergency room and receive medical attention. Her condition is called:
   a. factitious substitution.
   b. Munchausen's syndrome.
   c. malingering.
   d. factitious disorder by proxy.

8. Which of the following questions is not part of the Dissociative Disorders Interview Schedule?
   a. Were you physically abused as a child or adolescent?
   b. Do you feel physical pain that lacks a physical basis?
   c. Do you ever speak about yourself as "we" or "us"?
   d. Do you ever feel that there is another person or persons inside you?

9. Disturbances in the amount, quality, or timing of sleep are referred to as:
   a. hyposomnias.
   b. nocturnal dysfunctions.
   c. dyssomnias.
   d. parasomnias.

10. People with depersonalization disorder:
    a. have more than one personality.
    b. feel as though they are not real.
    c. forget details about personal identity.
    d. fabricate disturbance to get secondary gain.

11. The higher rate of hypertension in African-Americans compared to Whites is thought by researchers to be due to:
    a. lower physiological reactivity to stress.
    b. a tendency to express strong emotions.
    c. lower levels of Type A behavior.
    d. patterns of poverty and discrimination.

12. The inability to recall past events from a particular date up to, and including the present time is called:
    a. continuous amnesia.
    b. generalized amnesia.
    c. selective amnesia.
    d. psychogenic amnesia.

13. Disorders in which psychological conflicts are translated into physical complaints are the:
    a. anxiety disorders.
    b. dissociative disorders.
    c. personality disorders.
    d. somatoform disorders.

14. Legal experts and psychologists have found this reaction to be indicative of a true diagnosis of dissociative identity disorder in forensic cases:
    a. extreme distress and interference of symptoms in daily life
    b. emergence of new personalities during therapy
    c. stereotypical criminal personalities as alters
    d. moderate or little distress over symptoms

15. Mr. Warren has seen many physicians, complaining of difficulty swallowing, chest pain, and blurred vision. Medical examination yields no basis for his claims. Mr. Warren seems to have this somatoform disorder:
    a. factitious disorder
    b. psychalgia
    c. pain disorder
    d. somatization disorder

16. Which somatoform disorder is characterized by dissatisfaction and delusional preoccupation with the idea that some part of the body is ugly or defective?
    a. Briquet's syndrome
    b. psychalgia
    c. body dysmorphic disorder
    d. hypochondriasis

17. A man persistently views his mild headaches as an indication he has a brain tumor despite lack of evidence in support of his claim. This individual may be suffering from:
    a. conversion disorder.
    b. psychogenic pain disorder.
    c. somatization disorder.
    d. hypochondriasis.

18. In contrast to individuals with dream anxiety disorder, people with sleep terror disorder:
    a. have pleasant dreams which cause them to wake up.
    b. do not recall any dream or any unusual occurrences during the night.
    c. move and walk about in their sleep.
    d. usually experience the terror during REM sleep.

19. The central or core personality in dissociative identity disorder is referred to as the:
    a. cardinal personality.
    b. nuclear personality.
    c. alter ego.
    d. host personality.

20. The coping style that involves trying to improve one's feelings about the situation is referred to as:
    a. emotion-focused coping.
    b. problem-focused coping.
    c. cognitive coping.
    d. confrontive coping.

ANSWERS
IDENTIFYING DISORDERS

1. Hypochondriasis
2. Dissociative fugue
3. Conversion disorder
4. Circadian rhythm sleep disorder
5. Pain disorder
6. Body dysmorphic disorder
7. Sleep terror disorder
8. Dissociative identity disorder
9. Munchausen's syndrome
10. Primary insomnia
11. Somatization disorder
12. Depersonalization disorder
13. Primary hypersomnia
14. Malingering
15. Dissociative amnesia
16. Factitious disorder

MATCHING

1. a
2. h
3. g
4. n
5. i
6. l
7. m
8. d
9. j
10. k
11. b
12. o
13. c
14. f
15. e

ANAGRAMS

1. CONVERSION
2. PRIMARY
3. HYPNOSIS
4. FUGUE
5. DYSMORPHIC
6. TRAUMA
Final word=
MUNCHAUSEN'S

SHORT ANSWER

1. Dissociative identity disorder is linked to epilepsy, schizophrenia, and somatoform disorder.
The symptoms of dissociative identity disorder are not consistent over time.
The individual may try to cover up symptoms.
Dissociative symptoms may be mixed with mood disturbance or personality disorder.
The individual may be functioning at a high level and not appear to have a disorder.

2.

Context	What precedes an event can influence its effects; an unexpected stress (such as a loss) may be more stressful than one that follows a long period of preparation.
Internal qualities	Internal or personal qualities such as biological, personality, and cognitive vulnerabilities can influence a person's coping resources.
External resources	External or situational resources such as a social network and material resources can help buffer the impact of a stressful event.

3.
Localized
Generalized
Selective
Continuous

4.
a. Localized amnesia
b. Hypochondriasis
c. Pain disorder
d. Kluft
e. Trauma

Symptoms of conversion disorder
Conditions related to somatoform disorders
Dissociative disorders
Well-known experts who studied somatoform disorders
Explanations of somatoform disorders

5.

Disorder	Nature of physical complaint	Physical symptoms	Theorized role of psychological factors
Conversion disorder	Involuntary loss or alteration of bodily functioning.	No	Caused by underlying conflict.
Somatization disorder	Multiple and recurrent bodily symptoms.	No	Caused by underlying conflict.
Pain disorder	Pain.	No	Caused by underlying conflict.
Body dysmorphic disorder	Preoccupied with dissatisfaction over appearance of bodily part.	No	Unrealistic perception of appearance.
Hypochondriasis	Exaggerated concern over normal bodily reactions.	No	Acceptable way for finding help for other problems such as depression.
Factitious disorder	Physical or psychological symptoms are feigned.	No	Desire to be center of attention, nurtured, masochistic wish to experience pain.
Psychophysiological	Asthma, headaches, ulcer.	Yes	Psychological factors can initiate, aggravate, or prolong medical problems.

6.

a. The term "psychological factors affecting physical condition" replaces "psychosomatic" based on evidence that such disorders are not "in the person's head."

b. These conditions include situations when a person's physical symptoms are temporally linked to a stressful event. The simpler term "psychophysiological" has traditionally been used to refer to these conditions.

c. A stressful event can lower resistance to disease. Such an event can also aggravate symptoms of a chronic stress-related disorder. Current explanations propose that stress stimulates lowers immune activity, leaving the body vulnerable to conditions such as gastroenterological problems, infection, cancer, allergic reactions, and arthritis.

d. Research by McClelland suggests that the suppression of emotions can lead to harmful physical reactions and research by Pennebaker suggests that it can be physically beneficial to put emotions into words.
e. The Type C personality is a proposed personality type identified in cancer victims who cannot express their negative feelings toward others. This activation may lead to chronic arousal of the sympathetic nervous system and lowered efficiency of the immune system, which is involved in the body's natural protection against cancer.
f. People with a Type A personality are thought to be in a state of heightened activation, leading to high blood pressure and risk of heart and arterial disease.

7.

Type of gain	Positive aspect	Negative aspect
Primary	Avoidance of burdensome responsibilities.	Lost wages.
Secondary	Sympathy and attention from others.	Annoyance and anger from others.

8.

Disorder	Problem involved in treatment
Somatoform disorder	Avoid reinforcing the client's adoption of the sick role, but also provide support so that client accepts psychological treatment.
Dissociative identity disorder	Avoid inadvertent reinforcement of other personalities.
Other dissociative disorders	Avoid provoking a dissociative episode in the client by moving too fast through the uncovering of traumatic memories.

9.

Coping method	Example	Possible positive outcome	Possible negative outcome
Emotion-focused	Try to look at the event in positive terms, such as it will help the daughter "grow as a person."	The mother will feel better about the situation.	The mother will fail to intervene on the daughter's behalf, and she may get into more serious trouble.
Problem-focused	Talk to the daughter's teachers and guidance counselors to get at the root of the problem.	Changes may be implemented that help improve the daughter's behavior.	The mother may feel frustrated if she finds that no one at school can really help.

MULTIPLE CHOICE

10.

a.
Exercising before bedtime.
Drinking coffee within six hours of bedtime.
Useing his bed for activities other than sleeping.
No regular sleep schedule.
Worrying about his sleep problems.

b.
Simple educational intervention to improve his sleep habits.
Behavioral strategies such as relaxation, biofeedback, and cognitive self-control.
Stress management.

1.	c	6.	a	11.	d	16.	c
2.	a	7.	d	12.	a	17.	d
3.	d	8.	b	13.	d	18.	b
4.	a	9.	c	14.	a	19.	d
5.	c	10.	b	15.	d	20.	a

CHAPTER 9
SEXUAL DISORDERS

LEARNING OBJECTIVES

1.0 What is Abnormal Sexual Behavior?
    1.1 Discuss the issues involved in defining abnormal sexual behavior.
2.0 Paraphilias
    2.1 Explain the characteristic features of paraphilias, including exhibitionism, fetishism, frotteurism, pedophilia, sexual masochism, sexual sadism, transvestic fetishism, and voyeurism.
    2.2 Contrast biological and behavioral explanations of the paraphilias, including the concept of "lovemap."
3.0 Gender Identity Disorders
    3.1 Describe the features that characterize gender identity disorders.
    3.2 Discuss the possible causes of and treatments for gender identity disorders.
4.0 Sexual Dysfunctions
    4.1 Indicate the nature of sexual dysfunctions and their relationship to the human sexual response cycle.
    4.2 Outline the diagnostic criteria for sexual dysfunctions, including hypoactive sexual desire disorder, sexual aversion disorder, female sexual arousal disorder, male erectile disorder, female and male orgasmic disorders, premature ejaculation, and sexual pain disorders.
    4.3 Discuss the roles of biological and psychological factors in the cause and treatment of sexual dysfunctions.
5.0 Chapter Boxes
    5.1 Explain the nature of the relationship between pedophilia and childhood sexual victimization.
    5.2 Discuss the implications of sex reassignment surgery as a treatment for transsexualism.
    5.3 Evaluate the issues regarding "treatment" of homosexuality.

IDENTIFYING DISORDERS

Write the name of the sexual disorder in the blank at the left that fits the symptom described at the right.

1. _____ Intense urges and fantasies involving exposure of genitals to a stranger.
2. _____ A woman is unable to experience orgasm during sexual activity.
3. _____ A man cannot attain or maintain an erection during sexual activity.
4. _____ Strong recurrent sexual attraction to an object.
5. _____ Recurrent or persistent pain in the genitals during intercourse.
6. _____ A man reaches orgasm before he wishes during a sexual encounter.
7. _____ Active dislike of intercourse and other sexual activities.
8. _____ Sexual gratification derived from rubbing against unsuspecting strangers.
9. _____ Attraction to sexual situations in which satisfaction is derived from having painful stimulation applied to oneself.
10. _____ A man has an uncontrollable urge to dress as a woman to achieve sexual gratification.
11. _____ A woman is convinced that she is a man trapped in the body of woman.
12. _____ Uncontrollable attraction to children to the point that sexual gratification can be achieved only in their presence or while fantasizing about them.
13. _____ Attraction to sexual situations in which the individual dominates the partner to the point of causing the partner physical or and/or emotional pain.
14. _____ A man cannot experience orgasm during sexual activity.

MATCHING

Put the letter from the right-hand column corresponding to the correct match in the blank next to each item in the left-hand column.

1. ___ Behavior or attitudes associated with society's definition of maleness or femaleness.
2. ___ A condition in which a person is interested solely in deriving sexual gratification from a specific part of another person's body.
3. ___ One of the pair of researchers who first studied the human sexual response in the laboratory.
4. ___ Paraphilic behavior in which the individual derives pleasure from dominating or being dominated by a sexual partner.
5. ___ The representation of an individual's sexual fantasies and preferences.
6. ___ Sexual dysfunction in which the man is unable to attain or maintain an erection.
7. ___ A paraphilia in which the individual attains sexual gratification from exposing his genitals to others.
8. ___ Anxiety experienced by a person during sexual intercourse due to preoccupation with his or her performance.
9. ___ Type of pedophilia in which an individual with a normal history of sexual development becomes sexual with a child in certain contexts.
10. ___ A disorder in which the individual feels trapped in the body of the other sex.
11. ___ An individual's attraction to members of the same and/or the other sex.
12. ___ Type of pedophilia in which the individual maintains a continuous interest in children as sexual partners.
13. ___ Sexual dysfunction in which the man reaches orgasm in a sexual encounter before he wishes to.
14. ___ A paraphilia in which a man derives sexual gratification from dressing as a woman.
15. ___ Clinician who developed an integrative approach to treating sexual dysfunctions.

a. preference molester
b. sexual orientation
c. male erectile disorder
d. gender identity disorder
e. Helen Singer Kaplan
f. spectatoring
g. situational molester
h. transvestic fetishism
i. premature ejaculation
j. partialism
k. Virginia Johnson
l. gender role
m. sadomasochism
n. lovemap
o. exhibitionism

ANSWERS TO CASE THOUGHT QUESTIONS

Try answering each of the thought questions in boxed clinical vignettes in the chapter. Then read the responses provided here for each case and compare them with yours. If your answers are very different from those we have provided, you should then re-read the relevant sections of the text that pertain to the diagnosis exemplified in the case.

Exhibitionism (p. 272)	Fetishism (p. 273)
Ernie may find it easier to be in this position of "power" with a young person who is lacking the psychological and physical capacity of an adult. By engaging in exhibitionism, Ernie may be compensating for feelings of inferiority in his view of himself as a potent male adult.	Tom's behavior did not cause distress to himself nor did it directly hurt others. However, Tom was dependent on the fetishistic object for sexual gratification, apparently to the exclusion of other sexual behavior. It is unlikely that Tom's motivation for breaking into cars is for a reason other than to gain access to women's shoes; therefore, psychological treatment would seem more appropriate than imprisonment.

Frotteurism (p. 273) Bruce's behavior is a paraphilia because even though women may not be aware of his sexual actions toward them, they are still "victims." Further, Bruce is psychologically dependent on this behavior for achieving sexual gratification. Behavioral techniques such as extinction and covert conditioning would help Bruce to rid himself of this inappropriate behavior.	**Pedophilia (p. 275)** Kirk would be regarded as a situational molester, since his prior sexual development appeared to be that of a normal male interested in age-appropriate partners; he became a pedophile in the context of his stepdaughter. Amy will perhaps suffer from problems such as low self-concept, vulnerability to further abuse by other partners, sexual dysfunctions, substance abuse, difficulty establishing intimacy, and depression.
Sadism and Masochism (p. 278) Jeanne is actually at risk of being physically harmed by Ray's sexual brutality to her. Therefore, even though she may be a "consenting" partner, she is placing herself in physical jeopardy. Ray may have been neglected and yet harshly disciplined by his parents, so that he found a beating preferable to being ignored. He may have learned to associate pain with love by having been cuddled after having been beaten.	**Transvestic Fetishism (p. 280)** Phil does not harm anyone by his transvestic behavior, nor does he seem distressed. However, he is consumed by fantasies to cross-dress each day and engages in behaviors such as masturbating at work that reflect his inability to control his impulses. The goal of therapy would be to work toward helping Phil gain control over his behavior so that he is less impaired and less dependent on cross-dressing for sexual gratification.
Voyeurism (p. 280) As in the case of Bruce, the targets of Edward's paraphilic behavior are "victims" in that their privacy has been violated. In addition, Edward seems dependent on this behavior for achieving sexual gratification. Unlike someone who enjoys watching adult movies, Edward can derive pleasure only from observing people who are not aware that they are being seen.	**Gender Identity Disorder- Part 1 (p. 282)** Men who are transvestic fetishists have gender identities as men, unlike Dale whose gender identity is that of a woman. Dale has had a lifelong sense of identity as a female, and he is committed to changing his sex so that it coincides with his identity.
Gender Identity Disorder- Part 2 (p. 284) It would be important to ascertain Dale's overall adjustment, the extent to which he identifies himself as a female, and the strength of his commitment to surgery. Dale might be advised to explain to those close to him that his decision is based on lifelong discomfort as a male. Whether he informs new people depends on whether he feels he can trust others with this information.	**Hypoactive Sexual Desire Disorder (p. 287)** A loss of interest in sexual intimacy can reflect problems in a relationship. Sometimes when people become excessively involved in activities outside their primary relationship, it is an effort to avoid intimacy. If the difficulty lies in relationship problems, it would not be surprising if Carol were still sexually responsive, but not particularly interested in intimacy with her husband.
Male Erectile Disorder (p. 288) Brian seems to be spectatoring, meaning that he is so anxious about his sexual performance that he is impaired in his spontaneity. It is possible that he lacks knowledge about sex, which compounds his experience anxiety. Brian would benefit from exercises that help him reduce spectatoring. Reading about sexuality or consultation with a professional might help him regain control of his sexual functioning.	**Female Orgasmic Disorder (p. 289)** Margaret has gotten into a cycle in which she cannot reveal the true nature of her distress to Howard because she has not honestly communicated with him up to this point in their relationship. It will be important for Margaret to begin by telling Howard of her difficulties so that the two of them can seek professional help.

Male Orgasmic Disorder (p. 289)	Premature Ejaculation (p. 290)
Chen may be "spectatoring" so that he is highly self-conscious and anxious about his sexual performance. The difficulty Chen is having does not appear to involve relationship problems, as he has consistent difficulties across partners.	There is no evidence from Jeremy's case history of deep-seated conflict; instead, it appears that he has formed unfortunate negative associations to sexual situations. Spectatoring seems to be a problem for Jeremy, just as it was for Brian and Chen.

Vaginismus (p. 290)
Having a sensitive partner would not be enough for Shirley to overcome her difficulties, as her problem is severe and chronic enough to warrant intervention. The childhood experience of trauma could very well have caused Shirley to form a negative association to sexual intercourse.

SHORT ANSWER

1. Indicate the contributions and limitations of Masters and Johnson's research on human sexual functioning:

Contributions	Limitations

2. A client is distressed over the fetish he has about baby's diapers. Describe the following behavioral methods that could be used in treating this client:

Type of method	Description of method
Counterconditioning	
Aversive conditioning	
Covert conditioning	
Orgasmic reconditioning	

3. Describe what is considered "abnormal" about coercing a partner to have sex while tied down compared to having sex in an exotic place that both partners enjoy:

_____

_____

4.

a. Describe the four subtypes of sexual aggressors identified by Hall and colleagues, and summarize the descriptions and treatments recommended for each type:

Type				
Description				
Treatment				

b. Contrast the argument put forth by Nicholas Groth that pedophilia is motivated by a desire for power compared to David Finkelhor's position that sexuality is the primary motivation for the pedophilia:

Power explanation	
Sexuality explanation	

5. For each of the following somatic treatments for sexual dysfunctions identify the disorder it is intended to treat, the intended mechanism of action, and problems or disadvantages associated with each.

Somatic treatment	Disorder	Mechanism of action	Problems/Disadvantages
Administer progesterone			
Surgical implant of penile prosthesis			
Castration			
Sex reassignment surgery			
Hypothalamotomy			

6. Anne is living with her long-term partner, Mary. Describing herself as "traditional woman," Anne is interested in domestic activities and works as a manicurist. She and Mary have a sexual relationship, and this relationship is consistent with Anne's sense of herself as a woman. Based on this information, answer the following questions:

a. Is Anne's gender role masculine or feminine? Why?

_____

b. Is her gender identity that of a male or female? Why?

_____

c. What is Anne's sexual orientation? Is this consistent with her gender identity? Why or why not?

_____

7. Contrast physical and psychological causes of sexual dysfunctions:

Physical	Psychological

8. Identify which sexual disorder or problem is treated by each of the methods below:

Method of treatment	Sexual disorder or problem
Dilators	
Squeeze technique	
Stop-start technique	

9. Delineate childhood experiences that might result in the development of sexual disorders.

Disorder	Childhood experiences
Paraphilias	
Sexual dysfunctions	
Gender identity disorder	

WORD FIND

Circle the words defined below in this puzzle.

```
W L B T M F C I L E T O H C T
V O Y E U R A A P H R K V O B
A V U R E O H E R K A O A V Q
R E R E C T I L E R N E R E U
E M G C E T N S M A S T E R S
S A S F I E U T A D V O D T Y
A P D I E U L O T R E Y S G E
D O I N M R C A U O S A E H Z
I B C I H I D I R C T H C V W
S M F A K S D F E T I S H I R
T S C R N M B D I S C N I O Q
M O A O A L E W I N E S M N J
```

1. According to John Money, a disturbance in an individual's _____ is responsible for the development of a paraphilia.
2. In _____ sensitization the individual learns to associate unpleasant emotional states with the paraphilic behavior.
3. A sexual dysfunction in which a man is unable to achieve or maintain sexual arousal is called male _____ disorder.
4. Researcher who, along with Johnson, brought the study of human sexuality into the laboratory: _____
5. The paraphilia in which the individual derives sexual pleasure from rubbing his genitals against an unwitting stranger: _____
6. In the paraphilia called _____ fetishism, a person derives sexual gratification from dressing as a member of the other sex.
7. Individual who derives pleasure from inflicting pain on another person: _____
8. A person who derives sexual pleasure from secretly watching other people in a nude or partially clothed state, or having sex: _____
9. In _____ ejaculation, a man is unable to control his orgasmic response until the time in sexual relations that he desires.
10. Strong and recurrent sexual attraction to an object, without which an individual cannot achieve sexual gratification: _____

MULTIPLE CHOICE

1. Researchers have noted that this factor may increase the likelihood of sexual offenses in adulthood:
   a. early family conflict and abuse
   b. secure patterns of attachment
   c. highly consistent parenting patterns
   d. lack of physical or sexual abuse

2. Fetishism appears to develop in a way similar to exhibitionism in that:
   a. most people with fetishism were sexually abused as children.
   b. early life experiences result in a connection between sexual arousal and the behavior.
   c. brain damage early in life appears to cause certain paraphilias.
   d. these paraphilias are commonly associated with sexual dysfunction.

3. An individual who has recurrent, intense sexual urges and sexually arousing fantasies of rubbing against another person is referred to as a(n):
   a. voyeur.
   b. sadist.
   c. frotteur.
   d. fetishist.

4. Jackson has a normal sexual history; however, following the financial collapse of his company, he sexually molested the young daughter of his business partner. Jackson is considered a:
   a. preference molester.
   b. child rapist.
   c. paraphiliac.
   d. situational molester.

5. The most common physiological intervention for treating pedophilia involves:
   a. administering the female hormone progesterone.
   b. administering the male hormone testosterone.
   c. psychosurgery called hypothalamotomy.
   d. administering electroconvulsive therapy.

6. Bondage is a term associated with:
   a. sexual sadism.
   b. sexual dysfunction.
   c. fetishism.
   d. transvestic fetishism.

7. The phenomenon in which a man derives sexual excitement from the thought or image of himself as having a female anatomy or biological characteristics such as menstruation or the ability to breast feed is called:
   a. transvestic fetishism.
   b. autogynephilia.
   c. inorgasmia.
   d. autoeroticism.

8. Which of the following factors has a positive influence on the postoperative readjustment of people who have had sex reassignment surgery?
   a. the quality of the surgery itself
   b. the individual's marital status
   c. uncertainty about the decision
   d. poor adjustment prior to surgery

9. The term that refers to the degree to which a person is erotically attracted to members of the same or other sex is:
   a. sexual orientation.
   b. gender identity.
   c. gender role.
   d. transsexualism.

10. The disorder involving an abnormally low level of interest in sexual activity is called:
    a. a paraphilia.
    b. sexual arousal disorder.
    c. hypoactive sexual desire disorder.
    d. orgasmic disorder.

11. The condition in which a man develops erection problems after a period of normal functioning is referred to as:
    a. primary erectile dysfunction.
    b. secondary erectile dysfunction.
    c. hypoactive sexual desire disorder.
    d. sexual aversion disorder.

12. Dyspareunia is a condition that involves:
    a. psychological distress associated with a paraphilia.
    b. depression that accompanies a sexual dysfunction.
    c. involuntary spasms of the outer muscles of the vagina.
    d. pain associated with sexual intercourse.

13. A sexual behavior is considered a psychological disorder if it:
   a. is forbidden by state, local, or federal law.
   b. is viewed as unacceptable by society or an individual's culture.
   c. causes harm to others or distress to the individual.
   d. involves unconventional sexual practices.

14. Biological theorists contend that exhibitionistic behavior may be the result of:
   a. damage to the ventromedial hypothalamus.
   b. unconscious desires for the parent of the opposite sex.
   c. loss of nervous system control of sexual inhibition.
   d. a cultural emphasis on male dominance.

15. A woman is erotically obsessed with men's ankles to the point of exclusion of all other erotic stimuli. This woman's desires are illustrative of:
   a. partialism.
   b. sadism.
   c. frotteurism.
   d. voyeurism.

16. The behavioral intervention geared toward a relearning process in which the individual associates sexual gratification with appropriate stimuli is called:
   a. aversion therapy.
   b. orgasmic reconditioning.
   c. cognitive restructuring.
   d. sensate focus.

17. A radical surgical procedure designed to treat individuals with pedophilia involves the destruction of areas of which brain structure?
   a. the pituitary gland
   b the frontal lobe
   c. the hippocampus
   d. the hypothalamus

18. Research regarding the "conversion" of gays and lesbians has shown that these treatments are:
   a. are ineffective and may be harmful.
   b. more effective for lesbians than gay men.
   c. successful when used with medication.
   d. recommended by most therapists.

19. An active dislike of intercourse or related sexual activities is the main symptom of which sexual dysfunction?
   a. male erectile disorder
   b. sexual arousal disorder
   c. sexual aversion disorder
   d. hypoactive sexual desire disorder

20. Based on what you have read about Masters and Johnson's technique of sensate focus, in which perspective does this technique seem to be rooted?
   a. psychodynamic
   b. cognitive
   c. humanistic
   d. behavioral

ANSWERS
IDENTIFYING DISORDERS

1. Exhibitionism
2. Female orgasmic disorder
3. Male erectile disorder
4. Fetishism
5. Dyspareunia
6. Premature ejaculation
7. Sexual aversion disorder
8. Frotteurism
9. Sexual masochism
10. Transvestic fetishism
11. Gender identity disorder
12. Pedophilia
13. Sexual sadism
14. Male orgasmic disorder

MATCHING

1. l	6. c	11. b
2. j	7. o	12. a
3. k	8. f	13. i
4. m	9. g	14. h
5. n	10. d	15. e

SHORT ANSWER
1.

Contributions	Limitations
Dispelled myths about sexuality	Laboratory setting was artificial
Provided a scientific basis for understanding sex	Samples studied were non-random
Gave a humanistic orientation to sexual functioning	An implicit sex bias which pathologized women

2.

Type of method	Description of method
Counterconditioning	Substitute relaxation for arousal in the presence of baby's diapers.
Aversive conditioning	Present a punishing stimulus every time the client touches baby's diapers.
Covert conditioning	Teach the client to imagine being humiliated while masturbating with baby's diapers.
Orgasmic reconditioning	Have the client experience orgasm while in the presence of appropriate sexual stimuli.

3. "Abnormal" sexual behavior involves sexual activity that causes harm to another person or that causes the individual to experience distress. Coercing a partner causes harm to that person; two consenting individuals having sex in an out-of-the-way place is distressing to neither person, even though it may be atypical.

4.

a.

Type	Physiological	Cognitive	Affective	Sexual
Description	Experiences deviant sexual arousal patterns. Victims likely to be male children.	Plans sexual aggression. Victims likely to be acquaintances or relatives.	Lacks affective control, sexual aggression likely to be impulsive. Depressed victimizes children, and angry victimizes adults.	Long history of personality and adjustment difficulties. Use violence toward victims.
Treatment	Castration, hormonal treatment, and aversion therapy.	Victim empathy training and relapse prevention.	Cognitive therapy for depression or anger.	Cognitive therapy, social skills training, behavior therapy, and prevention in adolescence.

b.

Power explanation	A desire to over-power children. Need to overcome loneliness. Act out aggressive impulses.
Sexuality explanation	Emotional congruence. Sexual arousal. Emotional blockage with adults. Poor socialization.

5.

Somatic treatment	Disorder	Mechanism of action	Problems/Disadvantages
Administer progesterone	Pedophilia	Reduce sex drive by reducing testosterone.	Potentially damaging side effects. Lowers ability to respond to appropriate stimuli. May lead to false belief of cure. No change in object of sexual desire.
Surgical implant	Erectile disorder	Permits erection.	Invasive, possible psychological impact.
Castration	Pedophilia and other dangerous sex offenses	Reduces sex drive by eliminating production of testosterone.	Arousal still possible. Radical intervention. May not eradicate deviant fantasies and wishes.

Somatic treatment	Disorder	Mechanism of action	Problems/Disadvantages
Sex reassignment surgery	Gender identity disorder	Changes body to be consistent with gender identity.	Results not perfect and hormones still needed. Child-bearing potential is lost. Psychological benefits are mixed.
Hypothalamotomy	Pedophilia	Change arousal patterns by targeting source of these patterns in the hypothalamus.	Ethical issues. Destruction of brain tissue can have unintended side effects. May decrease sex drive but not preference for children.

6.

a. Anne's gender role is feminine because she defines herself as "traditional," and has "feminine" interests and job.

b. Her gender identity is that of a female because she views herself as a woman.

c. Her sexual orientation is homosexual. Sexual orientation is independent of gender identity, so there is no basis for an inconsistency between her gender identity as a woman and her sexual orientation as a homosexual.

7.

Physical	Psychological
Illness and disease. Anatomical abnormalities or problems with sex organs. Medications. Drugs.	Misinformation about sex. Spectatoring. Cultural expectations. Relationship problems.

8.

Method of treatment	Sexual disorder or problem
Dilators	Vaginismus
Squeeze technique	Premature ejaculation
Stop-start technique	Premature ejaculation

9.

Disorder	Childhood experiences
Paraphilias	Early associations between sex and inappropriate stimuli.
Sexual dysfunctions	Traumatization and abuse. Learning of negative attitudes toward sexuality.
Gender identity disorder	Reinforcement of cross-gender behaviors..

WORD FIND

1. Lovemap
2. Covert
3. Erectile
4. Masters
5. Frotteurism
6. Transvestic
7. Sadist
8. Voyeur
9. Premature
10. Fetish

MULTIPLE CHOICE

1. a
2. b
3. c
4. d
5. a
6. a
7. b
8. a
9. a
10. c
11. b
12. d
13. c
14. c
15. a
16. b
17. d
18. a
19. c
20. d

CHAPTER 10
MOOD DISORDERS

LEARNING OBJECTIVES

1.0 General Characteristics of Mood Disorders
    1.1 Define the nature of an episode as used to diagnose a mood disorder.
2.0 Depressive disorders
    2.1 Indicate the diagnostic characteristics of a major depressive episode, types of depression, epidemiology, and course of major depressive disorder.
    2.2 Enumerate the criteria used to diagnose dysthymic disorder.
3.0 Disorders Involving Alternations in Moods
    3.1 Describe the symptoms of a manic episode, the types of bipolar disorder, epidemiology, and course of bipolar disorder.
    3.2 Indicate the diagnostic criteria for cyclothymic disorder.
4.0 Theories and Treatments of Mood Disorders
    4.1 Explain the biological perspective, including approaches to theory and treatment that focus on genetics and biochemical abnormalities.
    4.2 Evaluate the psychodynamic perspective and its application to understanding and treating mood disorders.
    4.3 Describe the behavioral perspective and how it is used to treat and understand mood disorders.
    4.4 Outline the cognitive-behavioral perspective to theory and treatment of mood disorders.
    4.5 Clarify the nature of the interpersonal theory perspective and how it is used in treatment.
5.0 Suicide
    5.1 Describe the characteristics of people who commit suicide.
    5.2 Explain the prevailing approaches to understanding why people commit suicide.
    5.3 Indicate the nature of suicide prediction and prevention programs.
6.0 Mood Disorders: The Perspectives Revisited
    6.1 Contrast and integrate the current approaches to mood disorders.
7.0 Chapter Boxes
    7.1 Evaluate the issue of whether Prozac is an appropriate treatment for mood disorders.
    7.2 Contrast the approaches to understanding suicide in adolescents compared to the elderly.
    7.3 Outline the research demonstrating the effectiveness of interpersonal therapy for depression.

IDENTIFYING THE THEORY

Put the letter corresponding to the theoretical perspective in the blank next to each proposed cause of depression:

P= Psychodynamic   **C=** Cognitive-behavioral
B= Behavioral   **I=** Interpersonal

Perspective	**Cause of depression**	**Perspective**	**Cause of depression**
1. _____	Distorted attitudes and perceptions of experiences.	6. _____	Attributions of helplessness.
2. _____	Criticism and rejection by others.	7. _____	Loss of loved object.
3. _____	Feelings of guilt and abandonment.	8. _____	Lack of positive reinforcement.
4. _____	Negative view of self, world, and future.	9. _____	Perceived loss which diminishes self-esteem.
5. _____	Lack of intimate relationships.	10. _____	Disruption of customary routines or scripts.

MATCHING

Put the letter from the right-hand column corresponding to the correct match in the blank next to each item in the left-hand column.

1. ___ Wonder drug of the 90s.
2. ___ Lethargic and listless behavior.
3. ___ Medication most effective in treating bipolar disorder.
4. ___ Relatives with identical genetic makeup.
5. ___ Taking excessive responsibility for failures.
6. ___ Symptom of major depressive disorder.
7. ___ Treatment of depression that involves working through conflicts related to particular life concerns.
8. ___ Measurement of cortisol levels.
9. ___ Treatment of depression that involves changing dysfunctional thoughts
10. ___ Response to ECT.
11. ___ Chronic and less intense form of depression.
12. ___ Explanations that people make of the things that happen to them.
13. ___ A period of elevated and expansive mood.
14. ___ Chronic vacillation between states of euphoria and dysphoria.
15. ___ Variant of depression that has no external causes.

a. endogenous
b. attributions
c. cognitive restructuring
d. lithium
e. psychomotor retardation
f. manic episode
g. dysthymic disorder
h. monozygotic twins
i. DST
j. short-term dynamic psychotherapy
k. clonic phase
l. example of cognitive distortion
m. Prozac
n. dysphoria
o. cyclothymic disorder

ANSWERS TO CASE THOUGHT QUESTIONS

Try answering each of the thought questions in boxed clinical vignettes in the chapter. Then read the responses provided here for each case and compare them with yours. If your answers are very different from those we have provided, you should then re-read the relevant sections of the text that pertain to the diagnosis exemplified in the case.

Major Depressive Disorder (p. 302) Agitation, dysphoria, suicidality, loss of appetite, insomnia, heightened sensitivity to criticism. If Jonathan's depression were melancholic, he would experience a worsening of symptoms in the morning and also struggle with psychomotor changes, appetite disturbance, and excessive guilt. Seasonal depression would be indicated if his symptoms are more likely to occur during the same season of the year.	**Dysthymic Disorder (p. 303)** Miriam has not experienced a major depressive episode and her symptoms have persisted at a chronic level for the past three years. Her depressed mood causes Miriam to have interpersonal problems, remain socially isolated, and fail to meet her work obligations. Lack of fulfillment and success can lead to lower feelings of self-esteem and lack of social support.
Bipolar Disorder (p. 306) Isabel had an unrealistic real estate plan, was running for three days without sleep or food, and showed extreme irritability when others interfered with her plans. Isabel lost control in the banker's office and acted in outrageous ways towards those who were skeptical about what was clearly a flimsy plan.	**Cyclothymic Disorder (p. 306)** Isabel showed the full symptoms of a manic episode unlike Larry, who became hypomanic. Larry's symptoms are unlike Miriam's, in that Miriam did not experience mood alternations. Larry's mood shifts prevent him from experiencing a stable life and he may feel a lack of control over his mood that interferes with his daily well-being.

SHORT ANSWER

1. What are five factors that predispose a person to recurrent depression?

   _____   _____
   _____   _____
   _____

2. From the point of view of the person experiencing a manic episode, what are two appealing and two disturbing features of such an experience?

Appealing features	Disturbing features

3. What are three reasons for the Amish being considered especially suitable to study for research on bipolar disorder?

   _____
   _____
   _____

4. What three lines of specific evidence are used to support genetic theories of mood disorders?

   _____
   _____
   _____

5. Describe the evidence indicating an interaction of genetic and environmental contributions to mood disorders, as indicated by research on adult female twins:

   _____
   _____
   _____

6. What two facts challenge the monoamine deficit hypotheses of depression?

   _____
   _____

7. What altered biological rhythms are shown by people with major depressive disorder?

   _____
   _____
   _____

8. List two experimental methods for treating depression that involve altering biological rhythms, and explain the proposed method of action for each:

Treatment	Proposed method of action

9. In the case of Janice Butterfield's depression, Dr. Tobin ruled out the diagnosis of dysthymic disorder. What factors would enable a clinician to make such a differentiation?

    _____
    _____
    _____

10. Fill in the information in the chart below with the proposed mechanism of action, disorder for which it is applied, and problems involved in the use of each somatic treatment listed:

Treatment	Mechanism of action	Disorder	Problems
Tricyclic antidepressants			
MAOI's			
Prozac			
Lithium			
Electroconvulsive therapy			

11. Describe the theories of suicide listed below and the theorist who proposed the theory or the basis of support for the theory.

Theory	Description	Theorist or basis of support for theory
Anomie		
Communication		
Hopelessness		
Genetic		
Neurotransmitter		

LETTERBOX PUZZLE

Find the words that fit the definitions below each of the puzzles. The words may be formed by choosing one block from each column. You may cross out squares as you solve, because each box is used only once.

DE	OS	ST	O	N	VE
E	P	I	S	MI	DE
S	E	AN	S	OL	UM
D	P	RE	HY	RT	C
P	Y	AS	PA	SI	IC
M	EL	T	CH	O	AL

Clues:
- Period in which specific intense symptoms are present.
- Type of depression involving loss of interest in activities, symptoms in the morning, significant disturbance of appetite and extreme feelings of guilt.
- In major _____ disorder, the individual feels extreme dysphoria, has physical symptoms, experiences low self-esteem, and may be suicidal.
- Depressive disorder involving chronic sadness without a period of intense symptoms.
- Pattern of depression in which symptoms are worst during the fall or winter.
- Specifier used to indicate that a woman's depression follows the birth of a child.

E	CL	P	Z	L	L
C	U	R	O	A	A
C	OG	PH	TH	RI	IC
P	O	O	TI	YM	VE
B	I	O	O	SO	C
CY	R	NI	T	I	AR

Clues:
- Disorder involving intense alternations in mood involving manic and/or depressive episodes.
- Hormone involved in mobilizing the body's resources in times of stress.
- Medication used to treat depression by altering the serotonin system; considered the "wonder drug" of the 1990s.
- According to one theory, people who are depressed experience a _____ triad of negative feelings about the self, the world, and the future.
- Feelings of intense elation or positive mood.
- Disorder involving chronic alternations in mood from mild depression to hypomania.

MULTIPLE CHOICE

1. Suicide hotlines may not be effective because:
   a. they are often poorly funded and staffed.
   b. callers do not divulge their identity.
   c. they are staffed by undertrained people.
   d. people do not call when at highest risk.

2. A diagnosis of bipolar disorder requires:
   a. the experience of a depressive episode.
   b. the experience of a manic episode.
   c. a family history of mood disorder.
   d. normal premorbid personality.

3. The suicide rate is highest among white males aged:
   a. 15-24.
   b. 30-40.
   c. 50-65.
   d. 85 or older.

4. Which of the following factors indicates that a suicide case should be viewed as high-risk?
   a. an elaborate suicide plan
   b. low suicidal lethality
   c. low suicidal intention
   d. parasuicidal intent

5. People with cyclothymic disorder experience chronic:
   a. episodes of depression.
   b. episodes of mania.
   c. alterations from dysphoria to hypomania.
   d. unrelenting hypomania.

6. Which statement is true regarding the role of genetics in mood disorders?
   a. In families in which one parent has a mood disorder, between 60% and 70% of offspring are likely to develop a mood disorder.
   b. Among dizygotic twins, the concordance rate is between 45% and 50%.
   c. Among monozygotic twins, the concordance rate is between 65% and 70%.
   d. In families in which both parents have mood disorders, between 90% and 95% of their offspring are likely to develop a mood disorder.

7. A psychiatrist has determined that a client has bipolar disorder. Of the following, what kind of medication is most likely to be prescribed?
   a. lithium carbonate
   b. tricyclics
   c. MAOIs
   d. anticonvulsants

8. The popularity of fluoxetine (Prozac) as a treatment of depression is due to the fact that Prozac is:
   a. economical.
   b. impressively effective with few side effects.
   c. so aggressively marketed.
   d. targeted to a wide range of neurotransmitters.

9. According to Seligman's learned helplessness model, depressed people:
   a. view themselves as incapable of having an effect on their environment.
   b. take comfort in the attention they receive from others.
   c. tend to exaggerate their symptoms in order to get out of undesirable responsibilities.
   d. have negative views of self, world, and future.

10. Dr. Charney is a cognitive-behavioral therapist. She is least likely to use this approach:
    a. cognitive restructuring
    b. didactic work
    c. graded task assignments
    d. aversive conditioning

11. Catecholamine is to _____ as indolamine is to _____ :
    a. serotonin; norepinephrine.
    b. GABA; serotonin.
    c. norepinephrine; serotonin.
    d. dopamine; norepinephrine.

12. In an important NIMH study comparing the relative effectiveness of medications and psychotherapy, Elkin and his colleagues concluded that people with:
    a. severe depression benefitted most from cognitive behavioral therapy alone.
    b. mild depression benefitted most from small doses of antidepressant medication.
    c. severe depression benefitted from neither medication nor psychotherapy.
    d. mild depression benefitted nearly equally from medication, cognitive-behavioral therapy, and interpersonal psychotherapy.

13. In the textbook case of Janice Butterfield, Dr. Tobin noted that Janice's WAIS-R scores reflected her serious depression. Which of the following would have led Dr. Tobin to draw this conclusion?
    a. Lethargy caused Janice to receive a Performance IQ substantially below her Verbal IQ.
    b. Janice's vocabulary definitions were not particularly creative, thus causing her to receive a below average Verbal IQ.
    c. There was a negative correlation between Janice's IQ score and her MMPI-2 scores.
    d. Most of Janice's responses contained aspects of delusional thinking and bizarre associations.

14. Researchers find that there is a sizeable percentage of individuals suffering from depression who also have the symptoms of another psychological disorder. Which disorder is it?
    a. somatization disorder
    b. post-traumatic stress disorder
    c. anxiety disorder
    d. dissociative disorder

15. Researchers have proposed that the seasonal type of depression may be caused by alterations in biological rhythms due to seasonal variations in:
    a. caloric intake.
    b. temperature.
    c. norepinephrine production.
    d. light.

16. Central to early psychodynamic explanations of depression is the notion of:
    a. "loss" at an unconscious level.
    b. disordered thinking patterns.
    c. lack of positive reinforcement.
    d. regression to an egoless state.

17. Which of the following statements is true regarding the rate of depression in African Americans?
    a. It is generally higher than is found for Whites.
    b. The rates are highest for those in their twenties.
    c. The rates are highest for those in their forties.
    d. The rates of seasonal depression are higher than in Whites.

18. That depressed people may be hypersensitive to norepinephrine levels and that biochemical changes in their brains may have decreased their abnormal sensitivity to norepinephrine is related to the process of:
    a. synergism.
    b. down-regulation.
    c. catecholamine deregulation.
    d. up-regulation.

19. An alternate somatic treatment for individuals suffering from severe depression who may not be helped by medications is:
    a. dexamethasone therapy.
    b. acetylcholamine therapy.
    c. electroconvulsive therapy.
    d. tricyclic antidepressant therapy.

20. The therapy derived from interpersonal theory follows a set of guidelines derived from:
    a. case studies.
    b. empirical research.
    c. naturalistic observations.
    d. laboratory studies.

ANSWERS

IDENTIFYING THEORIES		MATCHING				SHORT ANSWER	

IDENTIFYING THEORIES

1. C
2. I
3. P
4. C
5. I
6. C
7. P
8. B
9. C
10. B

MATCHING

1. m   9. c
2. e   10. k
3. d   11. g
4. h   12. b
5. l   13. f
6. n   14. o
7. j   15. a
8. i

SHORT ANSWER

1.
History of past depressive episodes.
Recent stress.
Minimal social support.
Family history of depression.
Lifestyle, personality, and health behaviors.

2.

Appealing features	Disturbing features
Heightened energy	Irritability
Heightened creativity	Lack of judgment

3.
They have restricted lineage.
Careful genealogical records are kept.
Their religion prohibits drug and alcohol use.

4.
Higher concordance based on proximity of biological relationship, including clustering of disorders among families of probands.
Family lineage studies that identify specific chromosomal abnormalities.
Adoption studies showing higher concordance among biological than adoptive relatives.

5. Female twins with a genetic predisposition to depression who suffered a traumatic life event had a much higher rate of depression (15%) than female twins with no genetic predisposition to depression (6%). Female twins who did not experience a traumatic event had an equal rate of depression (about 1%) regardless of genetic predisposition.

6. Medications take at least two weeks to have effects.
There is no evidence of a relationship between antihypertensive medication use (which reduces catecholamine activity) and depression.

7. Altered REM patterns, decreased time between falling asleep and REM sleep, earlier awakenings, seasonal variations in symptoms.

8.

Treatment	Proposed method of action
Light therapy	Exposure to bright light reduces melatonin production by the pineal gland; this may relieve depression in some people.
Sleep deprivation	Altering a person's biological rhythm through sleep deprivation may alleviate depression and in some cases may increase the effects of antidepressant medication.

9. Duration of symptoms; intensity of depression; absence of psychotic symptoms.

10.

Treatment	Mechanism of action	Disorder	Problems
Tricyclic antidepressants	Increase monoamine activity	Depression	Take at least 2 weeks to have effect. Not effective for all depressions.
MAOI's	Inhibit MAO	Depression	Take at least 2 weeks to have effect. Potentially dangerous side effects.
Prozac	Increase serotonin activity	Depression	Possible risks of suicidality and increased impulsivity.
Lithium	Decreased catecholamine activity	Bipolar disorder	Potentially dangerous side effects. From client's perspective, interferes with "high".
Electroconvul-sive therapy	Not known	Depression	Short-term memory loss. Adverse connotations.

11.

Theory	Description	Theorist or basis of support for theory
Anomie	Feeling of alienation from society leads individual to experience suicidal wishes.	Emile Durkheim
Communication	Suicide is an attempt at interpersonal communication.	Edwin Shneidman
Hopelessness	Depression leads to unresolvable feelings of stress and hopelessness.	Aaron Beck
Genetic	Suicidality has an inherited component.	Higher rates of concordance of suicidality in identical compared to fraternal twins; adoption studies support the role of heredity.
Neurotransmitter	Physiological differences exist between suicidal completers and controls.	Suicide victims found to have lower GABA levels in hypothalamus; lower serotonin levels.

LETTERBOX PUZZLE

		MULTIPLE CHOICE					
Episode	Bipolar	1. d	6. c	11. c	16. a
Melancholic	Cortisol	2. b	7. a	12. d	17. b
Depressive	Prozac	3. d	8. b	13. a	18. b
Dysthymic	Cognitive	4. a	9. a	14. c	19. c
Seasonal	Euphoria	5. c	10 d	15. d	20. b
Postpartum	Cyclothymic				

CHAPTER 11
SCHIZOPHRENIA
AND RELATED DISORDERS

LEARNING OBJECTIVES

1.0   Characteristics of Schizophrenia
    1.1   Identify the phases of schizophrenia.
    1.2   Describe the symptoms of schizophrenia including disturbance of thought content, perception, thinking, language, communication, speech, behavior, negative symptoms, and social and occupational dysfunction.
    1.3   Enumerate the types of schizophrenia, including catatonic, disorganized, paranoid, undifferentiated, and residual.
    1.4   Contrast the proposed dimensions of schizophrenia, including positive-negative and process-reactive.
    1.5   Describe the course of schizophrenia.
2.0   Theories and Treatments of Schizophrenia
    2.1   Explain the biological perspectives on schizophrenia, including research and treatment that focus on brain structure and function, and genetics.
    2.2   Describe theories and treatment within the family systems perspective.
    2.3   Describe the perspective of behavioral theory and describe treatments that are based on this perspective.
    2.4   Explain vulnerability models of schizophrenia.
3.0   Schizophrenia: The Perspectives Revisited
    3.1   Indicate the current status of research and theories on schizophrenia and the probable direction of future work in this area.
4.0   Chapter Boxes
    4.1   Describe the controversies involved in determining whether individuals recover from schizophrenia.
    4.2   Explain the nature of the relationship between schizophrenia and social class.
    4.3   Evaluate the research evidence regarding whether delusions can be modified through treatment.

IDENTIFYING DISORDERS

Write the name of the disorder in which the symptoms described are the prominent features.

1.   _____   Disturbances in thought content, style, perception, affect, psychomotor behavior, and interpersonal relating ability.
2.   _____   Psychotic symptoms following a period of stress and lasting less than a month.
3.   _____   False belief that one's partner is having an affair or in love with someone else.
4.   _____   Delusions or hallucinations that others are trying to harm the individual.
5.   _____   False belief that another person is in love with the individual.
6.   _____   Mixed symptoms that do not meet the criteria for specific types of schizophrenia.
7.   _____   Severe disturbances involving bizarre posturing or psychomotor behavior.
8.   _____   False beliefs that one is being harassed or targeted by others.
9.   _____   Psychotic symptoms that lack any particular theme or basis of organization.
10.   _____   Psychotic disorder with symptoms of schizophrenia and mood disorder .
11.   _____   Disorder with schizophrenia-like symptoms that lasts between 1 and 6 months.
12.   _____   Disorder in which an individual is influenced by the delusion of a close one.

MATCHING

Put the letter from the right-hand column corresponding to the correct match in the blank next to each item in the left-hand column.

1. ___ Biological marker for schizophrenia involving visual tracking of a stimulus.
2. ___ Side effect of certain neuroleptics that involves uncontrollable shaking, muscle tightness, and eye twitches.
3. ___ A false perception involving one of the five senses.
4. ___ Treatment of schizophrenia in which individual is taught new ways of communicating and interacting with others.
5. ___ Behavioral treatment in which clients can earn rewards for engaging in appropriate social interactions and other daily routines.
6. ___ Term originally coined by Kraepelin to refer to the disorder that is now called schizophrenia.
7. ___ Swiss psychologist who defined the "Four A's" of schizophrenia.
8. ___ A deeply held false belief not consistent with an individual's cultural background.
9. ___ Model for explaining the inheritance of schizophrenia through contribution of several genes with varying influence.
10. ___ Parrotlike repetition of overheard words.
11. ___ German psychiatrist who developed a system for diagnosing schizophrenia based on "first rank" symptoms
12. ___ Period in the course of schizophrenia prior to the active phase of symptoms in which the individual's functioning progressively deteriorates.
13. ___ Biological marker for schizophrenia in which the individual must make a response such as pushing a button when presented with a certain stimulus such as a specific letter.
14. ___ Period following the active phase of schizophrenia in which there are continuing signs of disturbance.
15. ___ Measure of the degree to which family members criticize, express hostility, and become overconcerned about a family member with schizophrenia.

a. Eugen Bleuler
b. sustained attention
c. prodromal phase
d. echolalia
e. Kurt Schneider
f. social skills training
g. multi-factorial polygenic threshold
h. token economy
i. hallucination
j. tardive dyskinesia
k. residual phase
l. expressed emotion
m. dementia praecox
n. smooth pursuit eye movements
o. delusion

ANSWERS TO CASE THOUGHT QUESTIONS

Try answering each of the thought questions in boxed clinical vignettes in the chapter. Then read the responses provided here for each case and compare them with yours. If your answers are very different from those we have provided, you should then re-read the relevant sections of the text that pertain to the diagnosis exemplified in the case.

Schizophrenia, Catatonic Type (p. 338)	**Schizophrenia, Disorganized Type (p. 339)**
Maria is showing catatonic stupor and catatonic rigidity. Maria was showing signs of rapid deterioration prior to the development of catatonic behavior.	Joshua's language is incoherent, he converses with imaginary people, he shows inappropriate affect (laughing and crying), and his dress and general behavior are disorganized and bizarre. People like Joshua are found all too often among the homeless population who lack proper community-based treatment for chronic schizophrenia.

Schizophrenia, Paranoid Type (p. 339) Esther has the bizarre delusion that radio waves in the air can insert evil thoughts into her head. Also, Esther has auditory hallucinations with content that is consistent with her delusional beliefs. Unlike a person with paranoid personality disorder, Esther's beliefs are bizarre and delusional, and she experiences disturbances of perception in the form of hallucinations.	**Schizophrenia, Undifferentiated Type (p. 340)** Bruce shows signs of catatonic and disorganized schizophrenia, thus leading to the undifferentiated diagnosis. Catatonic symptoms include some peculiar bodily movements (e.g., staring for hours). Disorganized symptoms include incoherence, inappropriate affect, and other behavioral peculiarities. One might argue that Bruce is living as satisfactory a life as he can expect given the severity of his symptoms. Yet, he is only 24 years old, and might be able to achieve a more satisfactory life if given appropriate support and direction.
Schizophrenia, Residual Type (p. 340) Joyce still has some symptoms such as being preoccupied with the belief that her mother-in-law intends to harm her. Yet, her symptoms are not severe, nor do they interfere with her everyday life. Consider whether Joyce would stand to benefit from help with these occasional flare-ups of symptoms and whether therapy might provide her with additional support. In all likelihood, Joyce could benefit from support. It would also be beneficial for her to have a relationship with a professional who is alert to the possible reappearance of any symptoms.	**Brief Psychotic Disorder (p. 344)** Anthony felt a tremendous amount of pressure from his father. In order to maintain his grade point average, he abandoned socialization and failed to take care of his health. The low scores he received on his law school admission exam were the final provocation. Anthony showed symptoms of paranoid thinking, bizarre behavior, and extreme emotional instability.
Schizophreniform Disorder (p. 345) The symptoms shown by Edward are the same as those found in people with schizophrenia; technically Edward would not be diagnosed with schizophrenia because he has shown these symptoms for less than six months. There was no apparent stressor in Edward's life. Also, the duration of symptoms is longer than would be the case with brief psychotic disorder.	**Schizoaffective Disorder (p. 346)** The schizophrenia symptoms shown by Hazel include delusions, hallucinations, and thought disorder. The mood disorder symptoms involve feeling high, accelerated speech and bodily activity, sleepless nights, and erratic behavior. She stops taking lithium because she finds the experience of feeling high is enjoyable.
Delusional Disorder, Jealous Type (p. 347) Paul shows the symptoms of delusional disorder, jealous type that include obsession with the false belief that Elizabeth is sexually involved with another person. The only symptom shown by Paul is that of jealous delusions having to do with Elizabeth's possible infidelity.	**Shared Psychotic Disorder (p. 348)** Both Julio and Carmen have become caught up in the shared paranoid delusion that others do not like them and are intent on doing them harm. They engage in extreme behaviors that fuel their suspiciousness and cause them to seem very odd to other people. People who develop shared psychotic disorder usually have unstable personalities to begin with, so it is quite likely that psychological problems in some form would have become evident.

ANSWER GAME

This puzzle is like the popular television game in which contestants provide the question for answers within certain categories. To solve this puzzle, write in the question within each category that corresponds to each of the answers. The answers are arranged in approximately increasing order of difficulty so that a 100 point question is less difficult than a 400 point question. You may try playing this game with a friend, and see who receives the higher score.

Categories

Points	Theory	Treatment	Famous person(s)	Research Design
100	**A:** An explanation of schizophrenia that focuses on altered neurotransmitter functioning. **Q:**	**A:** A somatic form of treatment that causes seizures. **Q:**	**A:** French physician who first identified schizophrenia as a disease. **Q:**	**A:** Design used to determine whether people with identical genetic endowment have the same risk for disorders. **Q:**
200	**A:** Explanation of schizophrenia that focuses on disturbed modes of communication within the home. **Q:**	**A:** Therapeutic environment in which staff and other clients work as a community. **Q:**	**A:** Quadruplets in NIMH study of genetic contributions to schizophrenia. **Q:**	**A:** Design in which people are studied who are born of biological parents with a disorder but raised by non-disordered parents. **Q:**
300	**A:** Behavioral explanation that schizophrenia results when an individual is designated as having the disorder and then acts accordingly. **Q:**	**A:** Behavioral intervention in which clients learn to interact appropriately with others. **Q:**	**A:** Introduced the idea of a vulnerability or diathesis model of schizophrenia. **Q:**	**A:** Design in which people are studied who are born of non-disordered parents but raised by disordered parents. **Q:**
400	**A:** Model of schizophrenia that proposes an interaction of genetic vulnerability and environmental stress. **Q:**	**A:** Medications that have antipsychotic properties. **Q:**	**A:** American psychiatrist who was one of the founders of the Danish adoption studies. **Q:**	**A:** Design in which people born of disordered parents are followed over their lives or assessed on certain key diagnostic tests. **Q:**

SHORT ANSWER

1. List Bleuler's "4 A's" and relate them to the current terms or concepts that are used to describe the same phenomena:

4 A's	Current diagnostic term or concept

2. Place a number next to the following ideas regarding the nature of schizophrenia indicating their historical order:
    _____ Restriction of criteria for diagnosing schizophrenia to a few critical symptoms that are clearly psychotic.
    _____ Distinction between Type I and Type II schizophrenia based on the nature of symptoms and other critical signs.
    _____ Schizophrenia defined as dementia praecox and regarded as due to premature brain degeneration.
    _____ Suggestion made that certain "first-rank" symptoms must be present for diagnosis of schizophrenia to be made.
    _____ Disorder labelled "schizophrenia" indicating that it was due to a split of psychic functions.
    _____ Schizophrenia identified as due to a form of disease.

3. List and define the symptoms of schizophrenia and summarize the potential impact on the individual of each:

Symptom	Potential impact

4. Regarding the Critical Issue "Do People Recover From Schizophrenia?":

a. What was the term "in remission" intended to mean?

_____

_____

b. What were the negative aspects of the term "in remission"?

_____

c. Why is there more optimism now than there was in the early 1970s regarding the long-term outcome of schizophrenia?

_____

_____

d.   What two criteria can be used to define recovery?

_____

_____

e.   What is one problem associated with each criterion for recovery?

_____

_____

5.   Three ways of classifying schizophrenia were described in the text. Describe the rationale and arguments against each basis of classification.

Basis of classification	Rationale in support of this classification	Arguments against this classification
Paranoid/catatonic/-disorganized/resid-ual/undifferentiated		
Positive-negative dimension		
Process-reactive dimension		

6.   For each of the three disorders listed below, summarize the current explanations of the disorder and methods of treatment as described in the text:

Disorder	Current explanations	Treatment
Schizophreniform disorder		
Schizoaffective disorder		
Shared psychotic disorder		

7.   For these biological explanations of schizophrenia, describe the proposed mechanism of action, original evidence to support the explanation, criticisms about it, and current understanding:

Explanation	Dopamine hypothesis	Chromosomal abnormality
Mechanism of action		
Supportive evidence		

Explanation	Dopamine hypothesis	Chromosomal abnormality
Criticisms		
Current understanding		

8. For each of the following methods of studying genetic vs. environmental influences on schizophrenia, describe what it is intended to show and what the limitations of the method are:

Method	Purpose	Limitations
Family concordance		
Twin studies		
Discordant twin-offspring study		
Adoption study		
Cross-fostering study		

9. Place an "X" next to the term that does not belong with the others:

a. Transactional
   Double-bind
   Labelling
   Expressed emotion

b. Cross-fostering
   Increased ventricle size
   Abnormal PET scans
   Cortical atrophy

c. Token economy
   Neuroleptics
   Social skills
   Milieu therapy

d. Sustained attention
   Smooth-pursuit eye movements
   Event-related potential
   Schizophrenia spectrum

e. High-risk
   Diathesis stress
   Dopamine hypothesis
   Vulnerability

10. Answer the following questions regarding the case of the Genain quadruplets:
a. At what point in their lives did each of the sisters develop symptoms of schizophrenia?

_____

_____

b. What makes the study of the Genains so valuable in terms of understanding the causes of schizophrenia?

_____

c. What was the hypothesized role of Mrs. Genain in contributing to the illness of her daughters and why is it necessary to interpret her role with caution?

_____

d. How did the 1981 follow-up status of the four quadruplets compare with their status at the earlier testing?

_____

e. What are the implications of the results from the Genain study for the study of genetic and environmental contributions to schizophrenia?

_____

_____

MULTIPLE CHOICE

1. David Marshall's parents described to Dr. Tobin his gradual deterioration during late adolescence, suggesting that David was experiencing:
    a. prodromal signs of schizophrenia.
    b. the residual phase of schizophrenia.
    c. schizoaffective disorder.
    d. a delusional disorder.

2. The "four A's" which Bleuler described as the fundamental features of schizophrenia are:
    a. anomie, association, ambivalence, and autism.
    b. antagonism, affect, association, and autism.
    c. association, affect, ambivalence, and autism.
    d. affiliation, association, affect, and autism.

3. Smaller frontal lobes and limbic system structures are thought to relate to:
    a. the negative subtype of schizophrenia.
    b. the positive subtype of schizophrenia.
    c. the presence of schizoaffective disorder.
    d. the reduced production of dopamine.

4. Edgar believes that his heart is being eaten away by worms, a delusion that fits into the category called:
    a. somatic.
    b. persecutory.
    c. insertion.
    d. nihilistic.

5. Which of the following is not a recognized symptom of schizophrenia?
    a. disturbed interpersonal relating ability
    b. disturbed sleep patterns
    c. disturbance in sense of self
    d. disturbance of affect

6. Which term is used for a research design that studies children whose biological parents did not have schizophrenia but whose rearing parents did?
    a. index adoption
    b. schizophrenic spectrum
    c. multifactorial
    d. cross-fostering

7. The diathesis-stress model of vulnerability to schizophrenia proposes that:
    a. some people have a predisposition that places them at risk for developing a disorder if exposed to certain stressful life experiences.
    b. trauma or stress may affect a person's interaction with offspring in such a way as to cause them to be vulnerable to developing a disorder.
    c. a disorder can only develop in individuals who have been exposed to stress.
    d. the closer the genetic relationship to a person with a disorder, the greater the likelihood of developing that disorder.

8. Soon after beginning a new and stressful job, Jason began to act in strange ways, such as sending email messages to co-workers regarding life on other planets. After three months, Jason was given a medical leave and with treatment, returned to normal functioning. The most likely diagnosis for Jason would be:
   a. brief psychotic disorder.
   b. schizophreniform disorder.
   c. reactive schizophrenia.
   d. schizoaffective disorder.

9. The symptoms of schizophrenia are associated with the overactivity of neurons that respond to which neurotransmitter?
   a. norepinephrine
   b. GABA
   c. serotonin
   d. dopamine

10. Janet and Jeannine have a close but extremely paranoid relationship. Over the years they have come to fuel each other's delusional thinking. This condition is called:
    a. shared psychotic disorder.
    b. delusional disorder, jealous type.
    c. shared schizophrenia.
    d. delusional disorder, grandiose type.

11. Emil Kraepelin believed that "dementia praecox" resulted from:
    a. lengthy institutionalization.
    b. deterioration of the brain.
    c. disturbed parent-child relationships.
    d. impaired cognitive capacity.

12. Disorders involving the single psychotic symptom of false beliefs are called:
    a. shared psychotic disorders.
    b. schizophreniform disorders.
    c. delusional disorders.
    d. factitious disorders.

13. DSM-I and DSM-II's definitions of schizophrenia were:
    a. very broad and resulted in overdiagnosis.
    b. too specific and narrow.
    c. stereotyped against minorities.
    d. not based on theory.

14. The case of the Genain quadruplets who developed schizophrenia provided evidence regarding the:
    a. difference between Type 1 and Type 2 schizophrenia.
    b. role of dopamine in the development of schizophrenia.
    c. interaction of genetic and environmental factors in the development of schizophrenia.
    d. cross-fostering of schizophrenic traits among siblings.

15.′ Efforts by researchers to alter the nature and frequency of delusions in people with schizophrenia have shown that:
    a. successful treatment required two to three years of intensive therapy.
    b. the greatest success resulted from reality testing exercises.
    c. although delusions decreased, subjects became more depressed and anxious.
    d. verbal challenges were most successful in promoting change.

16. According to the downward social drift hypothesis of schizophrenia:
    a. there is a decrease in the amount of brain processing of social input.
    b. people with schizophrenia develop the disorder because of low social class.
    c. after people develop schizophrenia, their social class declines.
    d. the friends of people with schizophrenia abandon them after they are diagnosed.

17. Which type of schizophrenia is characterized by incoherence, loose associations, inappropriate affect and haphazard behavior?
    a. paranoid type
    b. undifferentiated type
    c. catatonic type
    d. disorganized type

18. Researchers refer to the symptoms of schizophrenia that are exaggerations or distortions of normal thoughts, emotions, and behavior as:
    a. positive symptoms.
    b. negative symptoms.
    c. anhedonic symptoms.
    d. hebephrenic symptoms.

19. Which dimension of schizophrenia provides a reliable basis for predicting the long-term outcome of the disorder?
    a. prodromal-residual
    b. paranoid-disorganized
    c. positive-negative
    d. catatonic-disorganized

20. The index of the degree that family members speak in ways that reflect criticism, hostile feelings, and emotional over-involvement or overconcern with regard to the individual with schizophrenia is referred to as:
    a. event related potential.
    b. expressed emotion.
    c. expressive threshold.
    d. affective index.

ANSWERS

IDENTIFYING DISORDERS

1. Schizophrenia
2. Brief psychotic disorder
3. Delusional disorder, jealous type
4. Schizophrenia, paranoid type
5. Delusional disorder, erotomanic type
6. Schizophrenia, undifferentiated type
7. Schizophrenia, catatonic type
8. Delusional disorder, persecutory type
9. Schizophrenia, disorganized type
10. Schizoaffective disorder
11. Schizophreniform disorder
12. Shared psychotic disorder

MATCHING

1.	n	9.	g
2.	j	10.	d
3.	i	11.	e
4.	f	12.	c
5.	h	13.	b
6.	m	14.	k
7.	a	15.	l
8.	o		

ANSWER GAME

Question Value	Categories			
	Theory	Treatment	Famous Person or People	Research Design
100	What is the dopamine hypothesis?	What is ECT?	Who is Benjamin Morel?	What is a twin study?
200	What is family systems?	What is milieu therapy?	Who are the Genain sisters?	What is an adoption study?
300	What is labelling?	What is social skills training?	Who is Paul Meehl?	What is cross-fostering?
400	What is diathesis-stress?	What are neuroleptics?	Who is Seymour Kety?	What is a high-risk study?

SHORT ANSWER

1.

4 A's	Current diagnostic term or concept
Association	Incoherence
Affect	Disturbance of affect
Ambivalence	Disturbance of motivation
Autism	Disturbed interpersonal relating ability

2. 5, 6, 2, 4, 3, 1

3.

Symptom	Potential impact
Disturbance of thought content: Delusions	Misinterpret behavior of others; form erroneous conclusions from daily experiences.
Disturbance in perceptions: Hallucinations	Images may be frightening and painful and are disruptive in daily life.
Disturbance of thinking, language, and communication: Disorganized speech	Difficulties in social interactions.
Disturbed behavior	Behavior looks odd to other people.
Negative symptoms	Loss of spontaneity and enjoyment in daily life, including the ability to experience pleasure from activities.
Social and occupational dysfunction	Lack of interaction with others causes loss of social skills which leads to further isolation; inability to keep a job influences standard of living.

4.
a. The term "in remission" was used to describe a person previously diagnosed as having schizophrenia not currently suffering from symptoms.
b. The term "in remission" implied that schizophrenia was in "hiding," waiting to reappear; with this diagnosis a person would never appear to have recovered from schizophrenia even though there may be no evidence of symptoms for years.
c. There is increased optimism in the 1990s compared to the 1970s regarding the potential for recovery from schizophrenia because there have been more rigorous research studies conducted and more precise definitions of schizophrenia.
d. Recovery can be defined in terms of (1) staying out of the hospital with no recurrent episodes and (2) a return to normal levels of social functioning.
e. Criterion (1) may be affected more by the availability of social support and insurance an individual has rather than the presence or absence of symptoms. A further complication is that a length of time must be agreed upon during which no psychotic episode must occur for the person to have "recovered." A difficulty with criterion (2) is that it may be difficult to arrive at a definition of "normal" social functioning.

5.

Basis of classification	Rationale in support of this classification	Arguments against this classification
Paranoid/catatonic/ disorganized/resid-ual/undifferentiated	Captures qualitative differences based on symptoms	Categories do not capture underlying dimensions of schizophrenia
Positive-negative dimension	Reliable system for predicting long-term outcome	Difficult to form clear-cut diagnosis and many clients have "mixed" symptoms

Process-reactive dimension	Intended to provide a useful system for diagnosis and estimation of prognosis	People with symptoms on reactive pole of dimension no longer regarded as having a diagnosis of schizophrenia

6.

Disorder	Current explanations	Treatment
Schizophreniform disorder	Biological links to schizophrenia as indicated by large brain ventricles, similar PET scans, and higher incidence in biological relatives	Antipsychotic medications, antianxiety medications, lithium, ECT, and psychotherapy
Schizoaffective disorder	Debate over whether disorder is a variant of schizophrenia or affective disorder	Lithium, antidepressant medications, antipsychotic medications, and psychotherapy
Shared psychotic disorder	Relationship issues in which dominant person feels isolated and seeks ally in weaker person who has come to rely on the other	Separation of the two individuals; therapy with submissive partner regarding vulnerability to domination

7.

Explanation	Dopamine hypothesis	Chromosomal abnormality
Mechanism of action	Increased dopamine activity.	Defect on a given chromosome underlies dopamine abnormality.
Supportive evidence	Antipsychotic drugs block dopamine receptors. Drugs related to dopamine increase frequence of psychotic symptoms.	Genetic mapping studies involving attempts to identify a susceptibility gene for schizophrenia have indicated several possible loci.
Criticisms	No difference exists between people with schizophrenia and normal individuals in dopamine metabolism.	Original findings have not been reliably replicated by other investigators.
Current understanding	Dopamine hypothesis may apply to Type 1 schizophrenia but not Type 2.	Researchers are still hoping to discover chromosomal abnormalities related to schizophrenia.

8.

Method	Purpose	Limitations
Family concordance	Relationship between proximity of biological relationship and concordance for schizophrenia.	Families share not only genetics factors but also the same environments.
Twin studies	Identical twins share same genetic endowment; concordance rate for schizophrenia reveals direct estimate of genetic contribution.	Identical twins share the same environment as well as identical genetic makeup.
Discordant twin-offspring study	Determination of whether offspring of discordant twins have higher concordance for schizophrenia provides further information on genetic determination of the disorder.	Still remaining unclear is why in the original discordant pairs one twin and not the other develops schizophrenia.
Adoption study	Rule out the influence of environmental factors in family concordance studies.	Adopting families may not be free of disorder and therefore not provide a "clean" environment.
Cross-fostering study	Evaluate the effect of environmental contributions to schizophrenia in the absence of genetic inheritance.	Very difficult to conduct due to small incidence of disordered adopting parents.

9. a. Labelling   Family systems explanations of schizophrenia.
    b. Cross-fostering   Brain changes.
    c. Neuroleptics   Behavioral treatments for schizophrenia.
    d. Schizophrenia spectrum   Biological markers for schizophrenia.
    e. Dopamine hypothesis   Concepts related to the vulnerability model of schizophrenia.

10. a. All showed signs of disorder by the time they were in their 20s.
    b. As identical quadruplets, they shared the same genetic makeup; it is unusual to find such a family. In addition, they were studied over the course of their adult lives.
    c. Mrs. Genain was hypothesized to have given conflicting and confusing messages to her daughters, and to pressure the more competent ones to conform to the characteristics of the sisters who had more severe disturbance. It is necessary to interpret Mrs. Genain's role with caution because it would be a mistake to place too much importance on the effects of parenting style on the development of schizophrenia.
    d. The four sisters changed in order of degree of impairment with Hester and Iris originally showing more impairment than Nora and Myra; in the follow-up, Myra and Iris showed less impairment than the other two sisters.
    e. The fact that they all developed schizophrenia is convincing evidence for genetic contributions to the disorder; but the fact that their symptoms emerged in different ways over the years of adulthood and that their relative degree of impairment shifted suggests an interaction of genetics with environmental factors.

MULTIPLE CHOICE

1.	a	6.	d	11.	b	16.	c
2.	c	7.	a	12.	c	17.	d
3.	a	8.	a	13.	a	18.	a
4.	a	9.	d	14.	c	19.	c
5.	b	10	a	15.	d	20.	b

CHAPTER 12

DEVELOPMENT-RELATED DISORDERS

LEARNING OBJECTIVES

1.0 Introductory Issues
    1.1 Discuss the controversies involved in the definition and diagnosis of development-related disorders.
2.0 Mental Retardation
    2.1 Identify the characteristics of mental retardation and the behavioral competencies associated with the different levels of retardation.
    2.2 Describe the causes of mental retardation, including the genetic and environmental factors, intervention, and prevention programs.
3.0 Pervasive Developmental Disorders
    3.1 Identify characteristics of autistic disorder and those of its subtype, autistic savant syndrome.
    3.2 Summarize current explanations of autistic disorder, psychopharmacological and behavioral treatments of autistic disorder, and the controversies associated with aversive treatment techniques.
4.0 Learning, Communication, and Motor Skills Disorders
    4.1 Identify the characteristics of learning disorders.
    4.2 Indicate the diagnostic features of communication disorders.
    4.3 Describe the symptoms of motor skills disorders.
    4.4 Summarize current theories and treatments of learning, communication, and motor skills disorders.
5.0 Disruptive Behavior Disorders
    5.1 Identify the characteristics of attention-deficit hyperactivity disorder.
    5.2 Describe the symptoms of conduct disorder.
    5.3 Indicate the diagnostic features of oppositional-defiant disorder.
    5.4 Discuss theories and treatments of disruptive behavior disorders.
6.0 Separation Anxiety Disorders
    6.1 Indicate the symptoms of separation anxiety disorder.
    6.2 Evaluate the theories and treatment of separation anxiety disorder.
7.0 Other Disorders that Originate in Childhood
    7.1 Describe the features of childhood eating disorders.
    7.2 Indicate the nature of tic disorders.
    7.3 Summarize the characteristics of elimination disorders.
    7.4 Identify the symptoms of reactive attachment disorder.
    7.5 Describe the diagnostic criteria for stereotypic movement disorder.
    7.6 Indicate the features of selective mutism.
8.0 Development-Related Disorders: The Perspectives Revisitied
    8.1 Compare the contributions of the major perspectives to the understanding of development-related disorders.
9.0 Chapter Boxes
    9.1 Evaluate the issues involved in the use of aversive treatment for autistic disorder.
    9.2 Discuss the factors affecting delinquency rates in urban areas.
    9.3 Examine the current research involving adults with attention-deficit hyperactivity disorder.

IDENTIFYING SYMPTOMS

Write the name of the disorder in which the symptom described is a prominent feature.
1. _____ Delay or deficit in a particular academic skill.
2. _____ Refusal to talk when a social interaction is expected.

3. _____ Impulsive, restless, aggressive, and unable to focus on a task.
4. _____ Significantly below-average intellectual functioning and adaptive behavior.
5. _____ Involved in delinquent and criminal activities without remorse for one's actions.
6. _____ Massive impairment in ability to communicate and relate emotionally to others.
7. _____ Hostile, argumentative, and generally rebellious toward authority figures.
8. _____ Distress when parents are not present, even for short periods of time.
9. _____ Severely handicapped communication and emotional relatedness combined with extraordinary skill in an area such as memory or arithmetic.
10. _____ Repetitive, seemingly driven bodily behaviors that interfere with everyday functioning and can cause injuries.
11. _____ In females, impaired cognitive and neurological development between 5 months and 4 years of age.
12. _____ Difficulty understanding and expressing certain kinds of words or phrases.
13. _____ Normal development for first two years with loss of cognitive and adaptive skills before the age of 10.
14. _____ Obvious problems of verbal expression.
15. _____ Adequate cognitive and language development with severe impairment in social interaction and restricted, repetitive, and stereotyped patterns of behavior.

MATCHING

Put the letter from the right-hand column corresponding to the correct match in the blank next to each item in the left-hand column.

1. ____ Abnormalities in this neurotransmitter system are thought to be a source of attention-deficit/hyperactivity disorder.

2. ____ Level of mental retardation in which individual can be trained but is unlikely to progress beyond second-grade skills.

3. ____ Disorder in which child regurgitates food after it has been swallowed, possibly eating the vomit after it has been spit up.

4. ____ Speech and language disorder characterized by mispronunciations, substitutions, and omissions of speech sounds.

5. ____ Form of mental retardation caused by chromosomal abnormality present from conception.

6. ____ Disorder of childhood in which child lacks control of bowel movements.

7. ____ In developmental _____ disorder, an individual has difficulty performing simple physical tasks.

8. ____ Medication found to be helpful in reducing symptoms of attention-deficit/hyperactivity disorder.

9. ____ Childhood disorder involving recurrent eating of inedible substances such as hair, paper, and string.

10. ____ Approach that is mandated by U.S. federal law to integrate children with mental retardation into public schools.

11. ____ Level of retardation in which individual can respond to a very limited range of self-help training.

12. ____ Form of tic disorder that involves involuntary uttering of obscenities.

13. ____ Form of pervasive developmental disorder shown by the title character in "Rainman," who could instantly make complex math calculations.

14. ____ Speech and language disorder characterized by limited vocabulary and use of grammatical structures.

15. ____ Disorder of childhood in which child lacks control over urination.

a. mainstreaming
b. pica
c. Tourette syndrome
d. coordination
e. catecholamine
f. encopresis
g. moderate
h. expressive language disorder
i. autistic savant syndrome
j. enuresis
k. Down syndrome
l. rumination disorder
m. methylphenidate
n. phonological disorder
o. profound

ANSWERS TO CASE THOUGHT QUESTIONS

Try answering each of the thought questions associated with the boxed cases in the chapter. Then read the answers provided here for each case and compare your answer with ours. If your answers are very different from those we have provided, you should then re-read the relevant sections of the text that pertain to the diagnosis exemplified in the case.

Mental Retardation (p. 372) Efforts would be made to involve her as centrally as possible in all of the activities of the classroom, using a special needs aide to assist the teacher. Depending on her level of retardation, Juanita would need considerable structure, with the provision of appropriate reinforcements. It is actually economically wiser to invest in Juanita's education so that she can become a productive member of society rather than requiring institutionalization or expensive community treatment.	**Autistic Disorder (p. 378)** Brian did not respond to his parents' efforts to play with and hold him during infancy, he clung to a small piece of wood which he carried everywhere, and spent most of his time rocking in a corner. His language was unusual, and his speech patterns involved echolalia and babbling. The fact that Brian is not aggressive makes it easier to implement behavioral techniques involving positive reinforcement aimed at facilitating social interaction. Nevertheless, therapy with people who are so seriously disturbed is difficult and challenging.
Attention-Deficit/Hyperactivity Disorder (p. 384) Joshua is extremely restless and distractible, he speaks quickly and his ideas are poorly organized, he is aggressive and socially inappropriate and unable to sustain attention on any activity for more than a few minutes. Although there are some unpleasant aspects of prescribing medications for children, Ritalin can help Joshua gain control of his disruptive behaviors so that he can have more positive experiences at home and school.	**Conduct Disorder (p. 385)** Bert has been involved in illegal activities even as a youth and shows defiance and lack of remorse when caught. Ideally, Bert should be treated within the mental health system, although in reality most of these cases end up being handled by the legal system. In answering this question, think about what type of psychological treatment might be beneficial for Bert.
Oppositional Defiant Disorder (p. 385) Unlike an adolescent with conduct disorder, Mindy has not committed any criminal or mischievous acts. Rather, her behavior involves defiance, negativity, and acting-out within the family. Mindy would probably benefit from a family intervention that focuses on the causes of her acting-out within the family system.	**Separation Anxiety Disorder (p. 390)** People with panic disorder with agoraphobia are afraid to leave the house due to fear of having a panic attack; Kira is afraid to be apart from her mother. Kira's mother has to be careful not to reinforce Kira's inappropriate behavior, while at the same time, she needs to recognize that Kira may not yet have the capacity to regulate her own behavior.

SHORT ANSWER

1. In what ways are the following pairs of items the same?
   a. Tay-Sachs disease and Fragile X syndrome: _____
   b. Phonological disorder and receptive language disorder: _____
   c. Echolalia and emotional unresponsiveness: _____
   d. Pica and ruminative disorder: _____
   e. Mathematics disorder and disorder of written expression: _____
   f. White noise and cold showers: _____
   g. Oppositional defiant disorder and conduct disorder: _____
   h. Albert Einstein and Henry Ford: _____
   i. Facial abnormalities and low birth weight: _____

2. Describe the possible role of biological factors as causes of each of the following development-related disorders:

Development-related disorder	Possible biological factors
Mental retardation	
Autistic disorder	
Language, communication, and motor skills disorders	
Attention-deficit/hyperactivity disorder	
Separation anxiety disorder	

3. Summarize long-term effects associated with each of the following disorders:

Disorder	Long-term effects
Autistic disorder	
Language, communication, and motor skills disorders	
Conduct disorder	
Attention-deficit/hyperactivity disorder	
Separation anxiety disorder	

4. Imagine that you are a parent of a child with attention-deficit/hyperactivity disorder. List three advantages and three disadvantages that you would consider if choosing medication such as Ritalin (methylphenidate) as a method of treatment?

Advantages	Disadvantages

5. Briefly describe the available behavioral treatments for each of the following development-related disorders:

Disorder	Behavioral treatment
Mental retardation	
Autistic disorder	
Learning, communication, and motor skills disorders	
Attention-deficit/hyperactivity disorder	
Conduct disorder	
Separation anxiety disorder	

ABC PUZZLE

_____

Fill in each of the blanks below which are in alphabetical order. The first letter of the answer is indicated at the beginning of the blank:

A_____ Disorder involving massive deficits in a person's ability to communicate and form emotional bonds with others.

B_____ Theoretical perspective on which aversive conditioning procedures are based.

C_____ Disorder in which a child becomes involved in criminal or delinquent activities and feels no sense of remorse.

D_____ Category of disorders that apply specifically to children.

E_____ Characteristic of autistic disorder in which the individual repetitively utters the sound of a verbalization.

F_____ Cause of mental retardation due to an abnormality on the "X" chromosome.

G_____ Category of causes of mental retardation due to deficits or abnormalities in a person's inherited potential.

H_____ Common term for a child who is incapable of sustaining attention on a task, becomes restless, and can irritate others by constant movement and aggressiveness.

I_____ Psychological variable on which categories of mental retardation are based.

J_____ Religious/ethnic background of people who are most vulnerable to inheriting Tay-Sachs disease.

K_____ Expert on autistic disorder who theorized that faulty mothering is the cause of the disorder.

L_____ Category of learning, communication, and motor skills disorders involving delays or deficits in academic areas.

M_____ Disorder in which individual suffers delays or deficits in acts involving coordination.

N_____ Historically renowned physicist who was a poor student in school and a failure in running the family farm.

O_____ A form of disruptive behavior disorder characterized by extreme stubbornness, rebelliousness, and resistance to authority.

P_____ Cause of mental retardation caused by failure (present at birth) to produce an enzyme needed for normal development.

Q_____ A child with selective mutism is very _____ because he or she refuses to speak.

R_____ Commonly known as "German measles," a disease that can cause mental retardation if the mother acquires it during the first trimester of pregnancy.

S_____ A disorder in which the individual shows a disturbance in the normal fluency and patterning of speech.

T_____ A rapid recurring involuntary movement or vocalization.

U_____ An environmental cause of mental retardation that is associated with high poverty levels.

V_____ Patterns of rising crime and _____ are seen as contributing to behavioral problems among inner city youth.

W_____ Use of these on cigarette boxes and alcohol labels is regarded as aiding in prevention of mental retardation.

X_____ Computer-aided versions of this radiological test can provide important information about brain abnormalities in people with disorders such as autistic disorder.

Y_____ Synonym for childhood and adolescence.

Z_____ Snoring noise made by weary students.

MULTIPLE CHOICE

1. Researchers studying adults with ADHD have found that many experience the following:
   a. other serious psychological disorders
   b. higher than average intelligence
   c. improved psychological adjustment
   d. lower cognitive distractibility

2. Form of mental retardation with brain changes similar to those found in Alzheimer's disease:
   a. Fragile X syndrome
   b. Tay-Sachs disease
   c. phenylketonuria
   d. Down syndrome

3. The most appropriate intervention for an individual diagnosed with PKU is:
   a. exposure to full spectrum light.
   b. a special diet.
   c. low dose radiation.
   d. neuroleptic medication.

4. Which of the following is a procedure that is used to detect chromosomal abnormalities in a developing fetus?
   a. amniocentesis
   b. chromosonography
   c. genetic mapping
   d. FAS screening

5. Mainstreaming is a term that refers to:
   a. the establishment of institutions that are devoted to educating people with disabilities.
   b. the placement of children with disabilities in foster homes where they can be appropriately nurtured.
   c. the integration into society of people with mental and physical disabilities.
   d. legislation that requires alcohol and tobacco products to carry warnings about potential toxic effects.

6. Which of the following statements is characteristic of Asperger's disorder?
   a. normal cognitive and language development.
   b. observed only in females.
   c. severe social and motor impairments.
   d. loss of adaptive functions before the age of ten years.

7. Eleven-year-old Jonah's speech is characterized by poor use of grammar and vocabulary relative to others of his age, although he is able to understand the speech of others. These are signs that he has this communication disorder:
   a. stuttering
   b. expressive language disorder
   c. phonological disorder
   d. mixed receptive-expressive language disorder

8. Michael is a third-grader who is often causing problems at home and at school. He is disorganized, messy, impulsive, inattentive, and accident-prone. In all likelihood, Michael would be regarded as having:
   a. attention-deficit/hyperactivity disorder.
   b. conduct disorder.
   c. oppositional defiant disorder.
   d. separation anxiety disorder.

9. This disorder is diagnosed in children who have great difficulty relating to others and express this either in avoidance of social interactions or in inappropriate familiarity with strangers:
   a. selective mutism
   b. separation anxiety disorder
   c. atypical autistic disorder
   d. reactive attachment disorder

10. In what context is a restrained time-out station used?
    a. aversive treatment for individuals with autistic disorder
    b. positive reinforcement for individuals with learning disorders
    c. behavioral treatment of hyperactive children
    d. rehabilitation of mentally retarded individuals

11. In explaining the hypothesized causes of ADHD, experts currently believe that it:
    a. develops as a result of inadequate intellectual stimulation.
    b. is a genetically acquired trait.
    c. develops primarily as a result of a disturbed family system.
    d. is biologically based, triggered by certain stressful environmental conditions.

12. The term used to describe behavior in which an individual has bowel movements in clothes or inappropriate places is:
   a. encopresis.
   b. enuresis.
   c. dyslexia.
   d. coprolalia.

13. The metabolic disorder that causes neural degeneration and early death, usually before the child reaches the age of four is called:
   a. Down syndrome
   b. Fragile X syndrome
   c. phenylketonuria
   d. Tay-Sachs syndrome

14. A syndrome involving mental retardation that develops in the child of a woman who regularly consumes excess amounts of liquor while she is pregnant is referred to as:
   a. Fragile X syndrome.
   b. alcohol dependence syndrome.
   c. Tay-Sachs syndrome.
   d. fetal alcohol syndrome.

15. Autistic children usually form attachments to:
   a. inanimate objects.
   b. pets.
   c. older siblings.
   d. their mothers.

16. CAT scans of the brains of individuals with autistic disorder reveal:
   a. temporal lobe malformations.
   b. low levels of cortical arousal.
   c. enlarged ventricles.
   d. lesions in the hypothalamus.

17. Norm has just started 1st grade but does not understand what his teacher means when she asks him to count to 10. He is also baffled by her requests to add or subtract numbers. Norm might be diagnosed as having:
   a. math phobia.
   b. mathematics disorder.
   c. expressive numeric disorder.
   d. dyscalculus.

18. Which of the following is the development-related disorder that is the precursor in childhood of antisocial personality disorder?
   a. overanxious disorder
   b. conduct disorder
   c. oppositional defiant disorder
   d. attention-deficit/hyperactivity disorder

19. In many ways, Sally seems like a typical teenager. However, she repeatedly argues with her parents, refuses to do what she is told and at times does things to annoy people deliberately. If this behavior pattern is relatively long-term, Sally might possibly have:
   a. conduct disorder.
   b. attention-deficit/hyperactivity disorder.
   c. rumination disorder.
   d. oppositional defiant disorder.

20. Seth is constantly moving his head and twitching his shoulders. He utters loud, abrupt noises that others regard as strange. These movement and vocal patterns are uncontrollable. The term used to describe Seth's condition is:
   a. Rett's syndrome.
   b. Sack's disorder.
   c. Asperger's syndrome.
   d. Tourette's disorder.

ANSWERS
IDENTIFYING SYMPTOMS

1. learning disorder
2. selective mutism
3. attention-deficit/hyperactivity disorder
4. mental retardation
5. conduct disorder
6. autistic disorder
7. oppositional defiant disorder
8. separation anxiety disorder
9. autistic savant syndrome
10. stereotypic movement disorder
11. Rett's disorder
12. mixed receptive-expressive language disorder
13. childhood disintegrative disorder
14. expressive language disorder
15. Asperger's disorder

MATCHING

1.	e	9.	b
2.	g	10.	a
3.	l	11.	o
4.	n	12.	c
5.	k	13.	i
6.	f	14.	h
7.	d	15.	j
8.	m		

SHORT ANSWER

1. a. Causes of mental retardation
    b. Communication disorders
    c. Symptoms of autistic disorder
    d. Eating disorders of childhood
    e. Learning disorders
    f. Aversive treatments for autistic disorder
    g. Disruptive behavior disorders
    h. Successful adults who had learning problems in school
    i. Characteristics of children born with fetal alcohol syndrome

2. a. There are several inherited causes of mental retardation, including phenylketonuria, Tay-Sachs disease, Fragile X syndrome, and Down syndrome.
    b. People with autistic disorder show abnormal EEG's, CAT scans, and MRI's as well as serotonin abnormalities.
    c. Damage to various brain sites during fetal development, birth, or early childhood.
    d. Some evidence exists for decreased activity in the frontal cortex involved in controlling attention and motor activity.
    e. Separation anxiety in children related to increased panic disorder in parents suggesting possible genetic link.

3.

Disorder	Long-term effects
Autistic disorder	Two-thirds of people with autistic disorder are unable to live an independent life as an adult.
Language, communication, and motor skills disorders	Increased risk of anxiety disorder, mood disorder, ADHD, conduct disorder, and adjustment disorder.
Conduct disorder	Marital difficulties, decreased occupational and educational opportunities, poor social relationships, alcohol use, poorer physical health, and antisocial personality disorder.
Attention-deficit hyperactivity disorder	Substance abuse, academic underachievement, decreased self-esteem, higher number of arrests (in men), and greater risk of depression (in women).
Separation anxiety disorder	Increased likelihood of developing anxiety disorder as an adult.

4.

Advantages	Disadvantages
Increased attentional control	Decreased sleep
Decreased hyperactive behavior	Decreased appetite
Increased positive social interactions with peers, teachers, and parents	Development of twitches

5.

Disorder	Behavioral treatment
Mental retardation	Reinforcement for appropriate use of speech and language, and the development of social skills; parents can be taught to reward a child for appropriate behaviors and to respond negatively to inappropriate behaviors.
Autistic disorder	Self-control procedures, relaxation training, covert conditioning, and in extreme cases, aversive therapy.
Learning, communication, and motor skills disorders	In the school context, more structure, fewer distractions, presentation of new material that uses more than one sensory modality at a time.
Attention-deficit/hyperactivity disorder	Teaching of self-control and changing of the contingencies in the environment; involvement of family in reducing child's destructive behaviors.
Conduct disorder	Teach appropriate behaviors such as cooperation and self-control while unlearning problem behaviors such as aggression, stealing and lying; use reinforcement, behavioral contracting, modeling, and relaxation training.
Separation anxiety disorder	Systematic desensitization, prolonged exposure, and modeling; contingency management and self-management can also teach the child to react more competently to a fear-provoking situation.

"ABC PUZZLE"

Autistic disorder
Behavioral
Conduct disorder
Development-related disorders
Echolalia
Fragile X
Genetic
Hyperactive
Intelligence
Jewish

Kanner
Learning disorders
Motor skills disorder
Newton (Sir Isaac)
Oppositional defiant disorder
Phenylketonuria
Quiet
Rubella
Stuttering
Tic

Undernutrition
Violence
Warning labels
X-rays
Youth
Z-Z-Z-Z (sorry, we couldn't find any "z" words in this chapter!)

MULTIPLE CHOICE

1.	a	5.	c	9.	d	13.	d	17.	b
2.	d	6.	c	10	a	14.	d	18.	b
3.	b	7.	b	11.	d	15.	a	19.	d
4.	a	8.	a	12.	a	16.	c	20.	d

CHAPTER 13
COGNITIVE DISORDERS

LEARNING OBJECTIVES

1.0 The Nature of Cognitive Disorders
    1.1 Explain the characteristics of disorders involving cognitive impairment.
2.0 Delirium
    2.1 Describe the symptomatic features and possible causes of delirium.
3.0 Amnestic Disorders
    3.1 Outline the types and causes of amnesia.
4.0 Dementia
    4.1 Indicate the symptoms of dementia, including memory loss, aphasia, apraxia, agnosia, and disturbance in executive functioning.
5.0 Alzheimer's Disease (Dementia of the Alzheimer's Type)
    5.1 Describe the epidemiology of Alzheimer's disease.
    5.2 Indicate the characteristic brain changes associated with Alzheimer's disease.
    5.3 Explain the stages of Alzheimer's disease.
    5.4 Indicate other physical diseases and psychological disorders that can lead to dementia resembling Alzheimer's disease.
    5.5 Contrast the biological and psychological perspectives regarding the causes and treatment of Alzheimer's disease.
6.0 Alzheimer's Disease: The Perspectives Revisited
    6.1 Discuss the prospects for improved understanding and treatment of Alzheimer's disease in the coming decades.
7.0 Chapter Boxes
    7.1 Indicate the problems involved in using chemical restraints to control the behavior of aggressive elderly patients.
    7.2 Discuss the nature of the discrimination faced by people with organic disorders caused by HIV and AIDS.
    7.3 Evaluate the research regarding caregivers of people with Alzheimer's disease.

IDENTIFYING DISORDERS

Write the name of the cognitive disorder in the blank next to the symptoms listed.

1. _____ Loss of memory for previously learned information or inability to learn new information.
2. _____ Progressive disease of the cortex involving memory loss, aphasia, apraxia, and agnosia.
3. _____ Patchy, stepwise deterioration of intellectual functioning.
4. _____ Cognitive and personality disturbances accompanied by involuntary spasmodic movements that eventually progress to the point of causing total disability.
5. _____ Symptoms mimicking Alzheimer's disease including depressed mood, disturbances in cognitive functioning, sleep and appetite, anxiety, suicidality, low self-esteem, guilt, and lack of motivation.
6. _____ Temporary disturbance in thoughts, level of consciousness, speech, memory, orientation, perceptions, and motor behavior.
7. _____ Deterioration of parts of the nervous system involved in control of motor movement.
8. _____ Degenerative disease that affects the frontal and temporal lobes of the cortex involving memory loss, social disinhibition, loss of motivation.
9. _____ Recurrent bodily seizures with associated changes in EEG patterns.
10._____ Rare neurological disease transmitted from animals to humans leading to dementia.

MATCHING

Put the letter from the right-hand column corresponding to the correct match in the blank next to each item in the left-hand column.

1. ___ Protein that forms the core of plaques found in Alzheimer's.
2. ___ Loss of the ability to carry out coordinated bodily movements.
3. ___ Discoverer of a form of language impairment in which the ability to produce language is lost.
4. ___ Physician who first identified senile dementia.
5. ___ Extreme muscle rigidity involving difficulty in initiating movement.
6. ___ Loss of memories for events prior to brain injury or damage.
7. ___ Neurological condition involving seizures and EEG abnormalities.
8. ___ Substance in the nervous system essential for the formation of acetylcholine.
9. ___ Loss of the ability to use language.
10. ___ Experimental drug used to treat Alzheimer's disease by altering levels of acetylcholine.
11. ___ Inability to recognize familiar objects or events.
12. ___ Discoverer of a form of language impairment in which comprehension abilities are lost.
13. ___ Loss of memories for events taking place after brain damage has occurred.
14. ___ Condition seen in neurons affected by Alzheimer's disease in which tiny strands form in the cell body.
15. ___ Loss or depletion of oxygen to the brain.

a. retrograde amnesia
b. Wernicke
c. epilepsy
d. aphasia
e. neurofibrillary tangles
f. agnosia
g. β-amyloid
h. anoxia
i. anterograde amnesia
j. tacrine (tetrahydroaminoacridine)
k. Alzheimer
l. akinesia
m. apraxia
n. Broca
o. choline acetyltransferase

NOT-SO-TRIVIAL PURSUITS GAME

This "puzzle" follows the lines of the popular board game in which players must answer questions within a set of six categories. Answer the questions below within these categories.

SL= Sports & Leisure   H= History
AL= Arts & Literature   G= Geography
E= Entertainment   S= Science & Nature

CARD 1:

SL	What disease makes it impossible for people to engage in finely tuned motor activities such as those required for athletics and many hobbies?
A	What is the name of a book written by Oliver Sacks describing people with various forms of brain damage or other neuropsychological disorders?
E	Who is the former actor who became President and was later diagnosed with Alzheimer's Disease?
H	Which neurologist discovered a form of aphasia in which the individual can produce but not comprehend language?
G	What is the country in which Alzheimer's disease was first discovered?
S	Which neurotransmitter system is thought to be most affected by Alzheimer's disease?

CARD 2:

SL	What is the metal in cooking utensils regarded by some as the basis for Alzheimer's disease?
A	Who is the author of *The Shattered Mind* which presented lengthy interviews of people with various forms of aphasia?
E	What communication systems are useful for providing support to family members of Alzheimer's patients?
H	What is the year in which Alzheimer's disease was first identified?
G	In which European river valley was there a clustering of families with Alzheimer's Disease?
S	What part of the brain is thought to be most affected by the degenerative processes associated with Alzheimer's disease?

ANSWERS TO CASE THOUGHT QUESTIONS

Try answering each of the thought questions in boxed clinical vignettes in the chapter. Then read the responses provided here for each case and compare them with yours. If your answers are very different from those we have provided, you should then re-read the relevant sections of the text that pertain to the diagnosis exemplified in the case.

Delirium (p. 399)	**Amnestic Disorder due to Head Trauma (p. 400)**
A comprehensive assessment including brain scanning and neuropsychological testing would be needed to determine whether Jack had suffered physical damage to the brain.	Harvey's disorder would be considered "chronic" at the point when it has lasted for a month without significant improvement.
It would be puzzling to see the change in Jack's behavior after the accident unless one were aware of the possible consequences of head injury.	In light of the fact that Harvey was sent to a rehabilitation facility, we can infer that he has suffered serious brain damage. In addition to the memory training he is receiving, Harvey could benefit from work with a clinician that focuses on coping strategies and readjustment to his memory loss.

SHORT ANSWER

1. Describe three approaches to diagnosing Alzheimer's disease, including their intended purpose and problems associated with each:

Diagnostic approach	Intended purpose	Problems

2. List the seven major physical diseases or disorders that can mimic Alzheimer's disease, the nature of the disease or disorder involved in each, and how its symptoms differ from Alzheimer's:

Physical disease or disorder	Nature of disease or disorder	How symptoms differ from Alzheimer's disease

3. Summarize the genetic theories for each subtype of Alzheimer's disease indicating the gene involved and the biochemical effect of the proposed genetic abnormality:

Type of Alzheimer's Disease	Proposed gene	Biochemical effect
Early-onset familial dementia (ages 30 to 60)		
Early-onset dementia as observed in descendants of families from the Volga River valley in Germany		
Early-onset familial dementia (ages 40 to 65)		
Late-onset dementia (age 65 plus)		

4. For each of the following forms of treatment or interventions for Alzheimer's disease, describe its goals and methods of implementation:

Treatment or intervention	Goals	Methods of implementation
Community services		
Medications		

Treatment or intervention	Goals	Methods of implementation
Caregiver support		
Behavioral treatment		
Cognitive-behavioral interventions		
Telephone information and referral services; computer networks		

5. According to the Research Focus, people with Alzheimer's disease and their families suffer a number of emotional strains and difficulties. Describe each of these with respect to:

Affected family member(s)	Emotional Difficulties
Spouse	
Children	
Alzheimer's patient	
Family as a unit	

6. How might each of the following indicators be used to differentiate depression (pseudodementia) from dementia due to Alzheimer's disease?

Indicator	Use in differentiating pseudodementia from dementia
Memory complaints	
Order of symptom development	
Nature of symptoms	
Exploration of recent life events	

7. Answer the following questions about the general category of cognitive disorders:
a. How was the term "organic" previously used in the context of psychological disorders?

_____

b. Why did the DSM-IV move to the term "delerium, dementia, amnestic and other cognitive disorders" rather than "organic disorders" to describe disorders caused by brain damage or disease?

_____

c. Provide four examples of psychological symptoms that can be caused by physical abnormalities:

_____   _____

_____   _____

d. What is the primary difficulty involved in diagnosing a cognitive disorder?

_____

_____

e. Why has epilepsy been inaccurately viewed for centuries as a psychological disorder?

_____

_____

8. Contrast delirium with dementia in terms of the following:

	Delirium	Dementia
Cause		
Course		
Primary symptoms		
Outcome		

9. Write in the blank next to the symptom the stage of dementia in which it first becomes evident using the following symbols:

F	=Forgetfulness	**MD**	=Middle dementia
EC	=Early confusional	**LD**	=Late dementia
ED	=Early dementia		

Stage	Symptom	Stage	Symptom
_____	Difficulty choosing clothes	_____	Becoming totally dependent on caregiver
_____	Mild forgetfulness and appropriate concern	_____	Complete deterioration of social skills
_____	Getting lost in familiar places	_____	Some date and time disorientation
_____	Forgets name of spouse	_____	Incapable of self-toileting
_____	Forgets telephone number	_____	Obvious denial of memory problems
_____	Denial of memory problems but with anxiety	_____	Loss of all verbal abilities
_____	Losing ability to handle finances	_____	Poor reading comprehension
_____	Occasional but not serious memory lapses	_____	Loss of ability to walk
_____	Withdrawal from challenging situations	_____	Family notices forgetfulness

MULTIPLE CHOICE

1. Which of the following statements is true about people with AIDS who develop dementia?
    a. Education can reduce fear and prejudice against these individuals.
    b. They are likely to encounter accurate knowledge and understanding from society.
    c. Attitudes toward their condition are not related to attitudes towards gays and lesbians.
    d. They receive preferential treatment in housing, employment, and health care.

2. The term "organic" in regard to psychological disorders was traditionally used to refer to:
   a. birth defects.
   b. physical illness.
   c. brain damage or dysfunction.
   d. refusal to eat pesticide-treated food.

3. Delirium is caused by:
   a. changes in the metabolism of the brain.
   b. intense levels of emotional stress.
   c. too much sleep.
   d. dietary imbalance.

4. Individuals with anterograde amnesia suffer memory loss:
   a. due to a traumatic emotional experience.
   b. as a result of epilepsy.
   c. for events prior to their amnesia.
   d. for new events that take place after the amnesia.

5. Controversy regarding chemical restraints for dementia patient centers on:
   a. the ethics and wisdom of using medication for restraint.
   b. whether such methods are as effective as physical restraints.
   c. the high cost of these medications when used on a daily basis.
   d. the fact that they are more humane than behavioral treatments.

6. Which symptom is not commonly noted in people with dementia?
   a. aphasia
   b. apraxia
   c. agnosia
   d. anoxia

7. Which of the following statements about Alzheimer's disease is accurate?
   a. The number of cases has decreased.
   b. Women have higher rates of this disorder.
   c. It affects 25% of the U.S. population.
   d. The rate is lowest in those over 85.

8. Clusters of dead neurons mixed together with fragments of protein molecules in the brains of people with Alzheimer's disease are called:
   a. amyloid plaques.
   b. neurofibrillary tangles.
   c. granulovacuoles.
   d. senillaries.

9. What is the name of the disorder which is a hereditary condition involving a widespread deterioration of the subcortical brain structures and parts of the frontal cortex that control motor movements?
   a. Parkinson's disease
   b. Huntington's disease
   c. Creutzfeldt's syndrome
   d. Brady's kinesia

10. Vascular dementia shows this characteristic pattern:
    a. pseudodementia
    b. patchy deterioration
    c. hydrocephalus
    d. sclerosis

11. Clinicians who provide services to families in which one member has Alzheimer's disease have focused increasingly on:
    a. shared environmental toxins.
    b. genetic predispositions.
    c. the problem of pseudodementia.
    d. caregiver burden.

12. Dependence on caregiver, delusional symptoms, and loss of awareness of all recent events first occur in this stage of dementia:
    a. middle
    b. early
    c. forgetfulness
    d. late confusional

13. Jeremy, a person with epilepsy, has seizures during which he loses consciousness, stops breathing for a short period of time, and experiences body jerking. Jeremy has what type of seizures?
    a. petit mal
    b. generalized convulsive
    c. partial
    d. focal

14. Annie is a 78-year-old woman seen in the E. R. who is delusional, unable to remember her last name, and slurs her speech. Her heart rate is rapid and she is sweating but she is not intoxicated. From what might she be suffering?
    a. amnesia
    b. Alzheimer's disease
    c. Huntington's disease
    d. delirium

15. Which of the following is the most common cause of amnestic disorder?
    a. chronic alcohol use
    b. chronic marijuana use
    c. head injury
    d. viral infection

16. Aphasia is defined as the loss of ability to:
    a. use language.
    b. recognize familiar objects.
    c. carry out verbal instructions.
    d. learn or remember events.

17. On autopsy, it is determined that a woman's cerebral cortex had degenerated and there were numerous amyloid plaques in the brain tissue. It is likely that this woman suffered from:
    a. Alzheimer's disease.
    b. epilepsy.
    c. pseudodementia.
    d. Tay-Sachs disease.

18. Chronic exposure to the fumes of house paints and petroleum fuels can lead to symptoms that mirror which of the following diseases?
    a. Alzheimer's disease
    b. AIDS
    c. Tourette's disease
    d. amnesia

19. While at rest, Ray's hands shake uncontrollably and his head jerks sideways. These are early symptoms of:
    a. Parkinson's disease.
    b. Pick's disease.
    c. Alzheimer's disease.
    d. Creutzfeldt-Jakob disease.

20. A link exists between Alzheimer's disease and which inherited disorder?
    a. Down syndrome
    b. autistic disorder
    c. attention deficit/hyperactivity disorder
    d. pica

ANSWERS

IDENTIFYING DISORDERS
1. Amnestic disorder
2. Dementia
3. Vascular dementia
4. Huntington's disease
5. Pseudodementia
6. Delirium
7. Parkinson's disease
8. Pick's disease
9. Epilepsy
10. Creutzfeld-Jacob disease

MATCHING
1.	g	9.	d
2.	m	10.	j
3.	n	11.	f
4.	k	12.	b
5.	l	13.	i
6.	a	14.	e
7.	c	15.	h
8.	o		

NOT-SO-TRIVIAL PURSUITS

CARD 1:

SL	Parkinson's Disease
A	The Man Who Mistook His Wife for a Hat
E	Ronald Reagan
H	Wernicke
G	Germany
S	Acetylcholine

CARD 2:

SL	Aluminum
A	Howard Gardner
E	Computer networks
H	1907
G	Volga
S	Hippocampus

SHORT ANSWER
1.

Diagnostic approach	Intended purpose	Problems
CT and PET scans, MRI	Detect structural brain abnormalities (CT and MRI) and metabolic defects (PET scans).	Measures not sensitive to brain changes specific to Alzheimer's disease.

Diagnostic approach	Intended purpose	Problems
Neurological and neuropsychological evaluations involving cognitive tests	Identify patterns of abnormalities indicative of brain damage or cognitive processes of memory and learning.	Can be used to help distinguish between pseudodementia and Alzheimer's disease but are not sensitive enough to Alzheimer's to make reliable diagnosis.
Mental status examination	Assess functional deficits associated with Alzheimer's.	Evidence of deficits in areas assessed by the examination is not sufficient basis for diagnosis.

2.

Physical disease or disorder	Nature of disease or disorder	How symptoms differ from Alzheimer's disease
Substance-induced persisting dementia	Brain damage resulting from exposure to toxins in the environment	Symptoms are progressive but occur in response to specific enviromental agents rather than disease.
Dementia due to head trauma	Brain injury	Similar to Alzheimer's but occur in a more sudden fashion.
Dementia due to HIV disease	Subtle deterioration in cognitive functioning due to AIDS	In addition to memory problems, symptoms include movement disturbances, delusions, hallucinations, extreme depression, apathy, and social withdrawal.
Pick's disease	Degenerative disease that affects frontal and temporal lobes of cortex.	Personality alterations precede memory problems.
Parkinson's disease	Neuronal degeneration of basal ganglia; deterioration of diffuse areas of cortex may also occur.	Main features are motor disturbances including akinesia, bradykinesia, shuffling gait, and loss of fine coordination.
Huntington's disease	Deterioration of subcortical brain structures and parts of frontal cortex that control motor movements. Degeneration of corpus callosum.	Main symptoms are involuntary spasmodic and often tortuous movements.
Creutzfeldt-Jakob disease	Neurological disease transmitted from animals to humans that leads to dementia and death.	Initial symptoms are fatigue, anxiety, appetite disturbance, sleep problems and concentration difficulties; disease progression results in loss of motor coordination, vision problems, and further neural disturbance.
Vascular dementia	Death of selected groups of neurons in cerebral cortex when clusters of capillaries in the brain are cut off by infarctions.	Patchy, stepwise cognitive deterioration.

3.

Type of Alzheimer's Disease	Proposed gene	Biochemical effect
Early-onset familial dementia (ages 30 to 60)	S182 gene on chromosome 14	Codes a protein embedded in a membrane of the neuron that might be involved in protein transport between neurons, and possibly connected with amyloid plaques
Early-onset dementia as observed in descendents of families from the Volga River valley in Germany	STM2 on chromosome 1	Seems linked to S182 gene
Early-onset familial dementia (ages 40 to 65)	APP gene on chromosome 21	Interference with disposal mechanism for APP might lead to accumulation of β-amyloid protein and eventual formation of amyloid plaques
Late-onset dementia (age 65 plus)	APOE on chromosome 14	The APo E ϵ4 allele codes for the E4 form of Apo E, which may damage the microtubules within the neuron that play an essential role in transport throughout the cell. This damage may occur through the destruction of the tau protein, which stabilizes the microtubules.

4.

Treatment or intervention	Goals	Methods of implementation
Community services	Maintain the individual for as long as possible at current level of functioning.	Diagnostic and medical assessment, counseling, support groups, financial planning assistance, and home care services; day care and respite programs to aid caregivers.
Medications	Offset the effects of the disease on the brain.	Vasodilators or metabolic enhancers to increase blood flow to the brain, choline-based substances to increase activity of acetylcholine; tacrine, which decreases the activity of cholinesterase.
Caregiver support	Help caregivers work through feelings of guilt and anger and other intense emotional reactions.	Insight-oriented psychotherapy.
Behavioral treatment	Maximize individual's ability to adapt to the environment and maintain independence.	Teach daily living skills (dressing, bathing, cooking, and social skills) and reduce disruptive behaviors (wandering and incontinence).

Treatment or intervention	Goals	Methods of implementation
Cognitive-behavioral interventions	Alleviate depression in afflicted individual and caregivers.	Focus on compensation for memory problems and help caregivers with feelings of depression caused by dysfunctional attitudes about their role in treating the individual.
Telephone information and referral services; computer networks	Provide caregivers with information as well as emotional support.	Informal sharing of help and information in a readily accessible format.

5.

Affected family member(s)	Emotional Difficulties
Spouse	Redefinition of intimate relationship as spouse assumes the role of caregiver; can feel emotionally drained and depressed.
Children	Caregiving child may become depressed and anxious; relationships between siblings become strained.
Alzheimer's patient	Sensitive to the concern of caregivers and fears becoming a burden on them.
Family as a unit	Feelings of guilt, obligation, and frustration develop in the family system as a whole and become heightened as the disease progresses, particularly when institutionalization is needed. On the positive side, families may "pull together" to deal with the crisis, and may experience emotional gratification at seeing the Alzheimer's patient respond to their caregiving efforts.

6.

Indicator	Use in differentiating pseudodementia from dementia
Memory complaints	Depressed individuals complain about their faulty memory, even though there is no physical basis for their complaints; the individual with Alzheimer's tries to conceal or minimize the extent of impairment or explain it away. As the disease progresses, the Alzheimer's patient may even falsely sense an improvement of memory functioning.
Order of symptom development	In depressed elderly people mood changes precede memory loss; the reverse is true for Alzheimer's patients.
Nature of symptoms	People with pseudodementia show classic symptoms of depression including anxiety, sleep and appetite disturbance, suicidal thoughts, low self-esteem, guilt, and lack of motivation. Their memory problems come on suddenly and they may have a history of depression. People with dementia experience unsociability, uncooperativeness, hostility, emotional instability, confusion, disorientation, and reduced alertness. The course of memory impairment is gradual and progressive.
Exploration of recent life events	Depressed elderly persons are more likely to have suffered a recent stressful life event; life events are not thought to be a factor in the development of dementia.

7.

a. The term "organic" was traditionally used in psychology to refer to physical damage or dysfunction that affects the integrity of the brain.

b. Movement away from the term "organic" was suggested in recognition of the fact that many psychological disorders have their origins in brain dysfunction. The current term more accurately describes the nature of the dysfunction in this group of disorders.

c. hallucinations
delusions
mood disturbances
extreme personality changes

d. It is difficult to differentiate symptoms associated with a psychological disorder from those arising in response to a physical disorder, even with the aid of sophisticated diagnostic technology.

e. Epilepsy has been misunderstood as a psychological disorder because people with this disorder may act in ways that appear odd or psychotic.

8.

	Delirium	Dementia
Cause	Change in metabolism of the brain.	Progressive degeneration of the cortex.
Course	Rapid onset and brief duration.	Slow onset and long duration.
Primary symptoms	Any or all of the following psychological changes: confusion, disturbance of consciousness, delusions, illusions, hallucinations, and emotional disturbances, as well as autonomic nervous system disturbance.	Loss of memory, language abilities, orientation, motor abilities, judgment, and social skills as well as emotional instability.
Outcome	Positive outcomes are possible such as natural recovery or positive response to treatment unless the delirium reflects a neurological disease or life-threatening condition.	Death invariably occurs due to the development of secondary physical illness.

MULTIPLE CHOICE

9.

ED	MD
F	LD
EC	ED
MD	LD
ED	LC
EC	LD
LC	EC
F	LD
LC	EC

1. a	6. d	11. d	16. a
2. c	7. b	12. a	17. a
3. a	8. a	13. b	18. a
4. d	9. b	14. d	19. a
5. a	10 b	15. a	20. a

CHAPTER 14
SUBSTANCE-RELATED DISORDERS

LEARNING OBJECTIVES

1.0 The Nature of Substance Abuse and Dependence
    1.1 Describe the nature of a psychoactive substance.
    1.2 Indicate the prevalence of substance abuse disorders in the U.S. population.
2.0 Behaviors Associated with Substance-Related Disorders
    2.1 Explain the nature of substance-induced disorders, including intoxication, withdrawal, and tolerance.
    2.2 Discuss the issues involved in defining substance abuse and dependence.
3.0 Alcohol
    3.1 Summarize the demographic patterns of alcohol use and impact on the family.
    3.2. Identify the physical and psychological factors that produce the immediate and long-term effects of alcohol on the body.
    3.3 Discuss biological and psychological theories of alcohol dependence.
    3.4 Summarize biological and psychological treatment approaches to alcohol dependence.
4.0 Stimulants
    4.1 Describe the effects of and physiological changes caused by amphetamines.
    4.2 Indicate the features involved in cocaine use and abuse.
    4.3 Explain the characteristics of caffeine-related disorders.
5.0 Cannabis-Related Disorders
    5.1 Indicate the behavioral and physiological effects of marijuana use.
6.0 Hallucinogen-Related Disorders
    6.1 Describe the types and effects of hallucinogens, including LSD and PCP.
7.0 Opioid-Related Disorders
    7.1 Outline the behavioral and lifestyle effects of opioid-related disorders.
8.0 Sedative-, Hypnotic-, and Anxiolytic-Related Disorders
    8.1 Indicate the short- and long-term effects of barbiturates.
    8.2 Describe the nature and effects of barbiturate-like substances.
    8.3 Outline the characteristics and effects of anxiolytic substances.
9.0 Other Substance-Related Disorders
    9.1 Describe the symptoms and disorders related to use of nicotine, inhalants, and anabolic steroids.
10.0 Substance Abuse and Dependence: General Treatment Issues
    10.1 Explain general principles pertaining to the causes and treatment of substance abuse and dependence including the role of biochemical mechanisms and psychological factors.
11.0 Substance Abuse and Dependence: The Perspectives Revisited
    11.1 Describe the integration of physiological and psychological factors in substance abuse.
12.0 Chapter Boxes
    12.1 Outline the variations by race and culture in patterns of alcohol use.
    12.2 Describe the research indicating the harmful effects of crack on prenatal development.
    12.3 Evaluate the evidence regarding the issue of whether humans are "programmed" for addiction.

IDENTIFYING THE SUBSTANCE

Write the name of the substance that is described in the right-hand column.
1. _____ A stimulant drug that was an ingredient of a popular soft drink during the late 1800s.
2. _____ The most widely-used illegal drug in the U.S.

3. _____ An opioid whose use had declined steadily from a peak in the 1970s but which appears to be on the rise again.
4. _____ Used appropriately as anesthetics, anticonvulsants, and sleeping pills, drugs in this category have high addictive potential.
5. _____ 10% of adults in the U.S. abuse or are dependent on this substance.
6. _____ A stimulant ingested daily by at least 85% of the U.S. adult population.
7. _____ Hallucinogen that was a central component of the nationwide drug culture of the 1960s.
8. _____ An inexpensive form of a stimulant drug whose use skyrocketed in the 1980s due to its availability on the streets and inaccurate perception of its risk.
9. _____ The yearly cost of abuse of this substance in the U.S. averages at least $100 billion.
10. _____ A category of stimulant drug whose legitimate medical use is appetite suppression, control of hyperactivity in children, and narcolepsy.

MATCHING

Put the letter from the right-hand column corresponding to the correct match in the blank next to each item in the left-hand column.

1. ____ Physiological and psychological reactions that can occur when a psychoactive substance is discontinued.
2. ____ Proposed subcategory of alcohol dependence theorized to be caused almost exclusively by genetic factors.
3. ____ The extent to which an individual requires larger doses of a substance to achieve its desired effects.
4. ____ A program that provides support and understanding for relatives and friends of people with alcohol dependence.
5. ____ Physiological factor that influences the extent to which a given amount of alcohol will have psychoactive effects.
6. ____ A psychological and physical need for a psychoactive substance.
7. ____ Alteration in behavior due to the accumulation of a psychoactive substance in the body.
8. ____ A pattern of drug use that creates significant problems for a person in everyday life.
9. ____ Physical condition involving autonomic system dysfunction, confusion, and seizures, caused by withdrawal from long-term heavy use of alcohol.
10. ____ Proposed subcategory of alcohol dependence caused by a hereditary predisposition interacting with environmental causes.
11. ____ Explanation of the biological mechanisms of alcohol that focuses on the changes in the body's cells caused by intake of alcohol.
12. ____ Psychological explanation of alcohol use proposing that a combination of beliefs about the effects of alcohol and reinforcement for these beliefs leads to alcohol dependence.
13. ____ Social movement that raised awareness of the impact of alcoholism on family members (abbreviation).
14. ____ The interpretation of a lapse by an alcohol dependent individual as a lack of ability to control drinking.
15. ____ Non-barbiturate substance with high abuse potential originally designed to replace barbiturates.

a. methaqualone
b. dependence
c. membrane hypothesis
d. Type 1 alcoholism
e. ACOA
f. intoxication
g. expectancy model
h. delirium tremens
i. tolerance
j. Al-Anon
k. substance abuse
l. metabolism rate
m. Type 2 alcoholism
n. withdrawal
o. abstinence violation effect

DIAMOND PUZZLE

The clues below are all for the "across" direction in this puzzle. Clue #1 is for the first row, #2 for the second row, and so on.

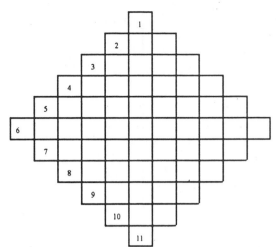

1. First letter of the abbreviation for a treatment approach for alcohol dependence which emphasizes commitment to group meetings, support networks, and spirituality.
2. Abbreviation for one of two enzymes that is responsible for metabolizing alcohol.
3. Use of a psychoactive substance in a way that places the individual at significant risk or harm in daily life.
4. Residential treatment program founded in the late 1950s based on the principle that substance dependent individuals benefit from a therapeutic community approach.
5. A drug that has THC as its active ingredient.
6. A drug used in treating alcohol dependence that is intended to reduce the desire for alcohol by acting on the GABA system.
7. Extent to which the individual can ingest larger amounts of a psychoactive substance without feeling its effects.
8. Stimulant drug thought to cause a "high" by blocking the reuptake in the nervous system of excitatory neurotransmitters, leading to stimulation of pleasure reward centers in the brain.
9. When the effects of cocaine wear off, a person is likely to experience a _____.
10. Hallucinogenic drug accidentally discovered by a scientist that became a central part of the 1960s drug culture.
11. Second letter of the abbreviation for the treatment approach for alcohol dependence in item 1.

ANSWERS TO CASE THOUGHT QUESTIONS

Try answering each of the thought questions in boxed clinical vignettes in the chapter. Then read the responses provided here for each case and compare them with yours. If your answers are very different from those we have provided, you should then re-read the relevant sections of the text that pertain to the diagnosis exemplified in the case.

Alcohol Dependence (p. 427)	**A mphetamine Dependence (p. 436)**
Rhona's drinking would constitute dependence because she increased her tolerance to alcohol, placed herself and others at risk (because of her driving), and denies that she has a drinking problem even though others in her life insist that she does.	Catherine would be regarded as dependent on amphetamines because she appears to have a psychological need for the substance and she is experiencing a number of ill effects in her daily life due to the use of the substance.
After her children left home, Rhona felt a void which she did not know how to fill. In addition, there is a history of alcoholism in Rhona's family, meaning that she might have a genetic vulnerability. It is also possible that in her family she learned to view alcohol as a means of coping with stress.	As indicated in the Critical Issue box, addictive behaviors may occur together in certain individuals, but there is no evidence to suggest that Catherine would show a particular pattern of personality traits.

Caffeine Intoxication (p. 440)	Cannabis (Marijuana) Dependence (p. 441)
Because she was in a state of agitation over her exams, Carla may have reacted more intensely to the high levels of caffeine she was ingesting. The physical symptoms of caffeine intoxication detected by Carla's physician were restlessness, twitching muscles, flushed face, stomach disturbance, and heart irregularities.	It appears that Gary's pattern of heavy marijuana use resulted more from experiences he had during college rather than his premorbid personality. Gary clearly needs professional help and his parents could benefit from consultation with experts in this field. In all likelihood, they would be advised to confront Gary and to change their behavior so that Gary has more incentive to get on with his life.
Hallucinogen (LSD) Dependence (p.442)	Opioid (Heroin) Dependence (p. 444)
Candace has often shown signs of hallucinogen intoxication and on more than one occasion her use of hallucinogens has placed her at risk. Candace may experience flashbacks months or even years after she has stopped taking LSD.	Jimmy runs a number of significant health risks associated with his lifestyle, including infections from needle sharing, damages to the veins and nasal passages, overdose, and most seriously AIDS. The prognosis for Jimmy's condition is not good as this disorder is very resistant to treatment.

SHORT ANSWER

1. List six types of medications used in the treatment of alcohol dependence and the intended effect of each medication.

Medication	Intent

2. For each of the following psychoactive substances, describe: (a) its subjective effects, (b) whether it has potential for tolerance and dependence, (c) whether there are withdrawal effects when it is discontinued, and (d) risks or long-term effects (apart from the dangers associated with withdrawal):

Psychoactive Substance	Subjective effects	Tolerance and dependence	With-drawal	Risks or long-term effects
Alcohol		Yes/No	Yes/No	
Amphetamines		Yes/No	Yes/No	
Cocaine		Yes/No	Yes/No	

Psychoactive Substance	Subjective effects	Tolerance and dependence	Withdrawal	Risks or long-term effects
Cannabis (Marijuana)		Not known	Yes/No	
Hallucinogens		Information not in text.		
Opioids		Yes/No	Yes/No	
Barbiturates		Yes/No	Yes/No	
Barbiturate like substances		Yes/No	Not discussed in text.	
Anxiolytics		Yes/No	Yes/No	

3. Link the terms in the left-hand column with the terms on the right by drawing a line from the term on the left to the matching term on the right. Explain how they are related to each other on the line that matches the term on the left:

How terms are related:

Wernicke	Caffeine	_____
Cue exposure	Enkephalins	_____
Cocaine	Withdrawal	_____
Endorphins	Relapse prevention	_____
Tolerance	Korsakoff	_____

4. Discuss the kinds of risks or accidents that result from the abuse of alcohol (be as specific as you can):

_____

_____

_____

5. Summarize the evidence for a biological theory of alcohol dependence in terms of each of the following areas of investigation:

Area of investigation	Available evidence
Patterns of inheritance	

Area of investigation	Available evidence
Biological markers	
Neurotransmitter functioning	
Search for an "alcohol" gene	

6. What are four obstacles that stand in the way of recovery for substance abusers?

_____   _____

_____   _____

7.

a. What is the central assumption of the relapse prevention model?

_____

_____

b. Four areas of focus involved in the relapse prevention model for treating alcohol dependence are:

_____   _____

_____   _____

c. What are the two central assumptions of Alcoholics Anonymous?

_____   _____

d. What four principles of treatment are similar in both the relapse prevention model and Alcoholics Anonymous?

_____   _____

_____   _____

e. In what two approaches to treatment does relapse prevention differ from Alcoholics Anonymous?

Alcoholics Anonymous	Relapse prevention

MULTIPLE CHOICE

1. Jared has found that he needs to drink 4 or 5 beers to achieve the level of relaxation that he was able to achieve with only two beers a year ago. This phenomenon is called:
    a. withdrawal.
    b. intoxication.
    c. potentiation.
    d. tolerance.

2. Which of the following is not associated with the rate at which alcohol is absorbed into the bloodstream?
    a. concentration of alcohol in a beverage
    b. time of day when alcohol is consumed
    c. metabolic rate of the individual
    d. mixing a carbonated beverage with alcohol

3. Which of the following has contributed to the hypothesis of a genetic link in the development of alcoholism?
    a. Sons of alcoholics are four times more likely to become alcoholic than sons of nonalcoholics.
    b. Daughters of alcoholics are three times more likely to become alcoholic than daughters of nonalcoholics.
    c. Fraternal twins have a higher concordance rate for alcoholism than identical twins.
    d. Children of alcoholics have a stronger reaction to alcohol than children of nonalcoholics.

4. Marianne takes a medication that gives her a headache, nausea, and other unpleasant symptoms each time she has alcohol. This medication is:
   a. disulfiram.
   b. nalxetrone.
   c. acamprosate.
   d. aldehyde.

5. Compared to amphetamines, the stimulating effects of cocaine are:
   a. longer but less intense.
   b. shorter but more intense.
   c. longer but more intense.
   d. similar in duration and intensity.

6. This term describes the experience in which a cocaine user develops convulsions because the brain's threshold for seizures has been lowered by repeated exposure:
   a. tolerance
   b. intoxication
   c. kindling
   d. potentiation

7. Cross-cultural research on patterns of alcohol use and abuse has shown that:
   a. rates of alcohol abuse are remarkably stable across cultures.
   b. Asian societies discourage alcohol use among men.
   c. prevalence rates are highest among the Amish in America.
   d. cultural and social deprivations can contribute to high rates of abuse.

8. Opioids are also known as:
   a. narcotics.
   b. hallucinogens.
   c. sedatives
   d. hypnotics.

9. The most frequently used drug in the category of barbiturate-like subances is:
   a. clonazepam.
   b. secobarbital.
   c. diazepam.
   d. methaqualone.

10. Which of the following statements is true regarding research on babies whose mothers used crack cocaine when pregnant?
    a. It is difficult to separate the effects of crack from those of other substances.
    b. These infants have higher birth weight and larger head size.
    c. Early intervention cannot alter the developmental course of a crack baby's life.
    d. Withdrawal effects are shown in the infants for at least the first year of life.

11. What is the term used for programs which are intended to minimize the physiological changes associated with withdrawal from substances?
    a. milieu
    b. therapeutic community
    c. Alcoholics Anonymous
    d. detoxification

12. Psychologists who have tried to validate the existence of an "addictive personality" have found that:
    a. this construct cannot be clearly identified.
    b. such individuals are unlikely to be depressed.
    c. they are addicted to substances but not food.
    d. their personality is linked to physiological factors.

13. The physical and psychological changes that accompany discontinuation of a psychoactive substance are referred to as:
    a. tolerance.
    b. intoxication.
    c. withdrawal.
    d. potentiation.

14. When two or more psychoactive substances are combined, the intoxicant effect can be greater than the effect due to each substance acting alone, a situation referred to as:
    a. sedation.
    b. inebriation.
    c. metabolism.
    d. potentiation.

15. Paul is a chronic alcoholic with dementia. He also has difficulties remembering past events and forming new memories. He suffers from:
    a. Type 1 Alcoholism.
    b. Alzheimer's disease.
    c. Wernicke's disease.
    d. Korsakoff's syndrome.

16. Joyce is alcohol dependent and trying to abstain from drinking. However, she went to a party, broke down, and had a drink. According to the expectancy model, how should she view this behavior?
    a. She should view it as a sign of a character flaw.
    b. She should view it as a sign of personal weakness.
    c. She should not view it as a result of social pressure.
    d. She should not view it as a loss of self-control.

17. Which treatment program is heavily grounded in spirituality?
    a. Alcoholics Anonymous
    b. cue exposure method
    c. relapse prevention therapy
    d. detoxification

18. Amphetamines have their effect by enhancing the action of which neurotransmitter?
    a. serotonin
    b. norepinephrine
    c. GABA
    d. dopamine

19. Spontaneous hallucinations, delusions, or disturbances in mood which are not the result of ingestion of a hallucinogen are called:
    a. psychotic breaks.
    b. delirium tremens.
    c. flashbacks.
    d. illusory spasms.

20. Enkephalins and endorphins are:
    a. natural pain-killing substances produced by the brain.
    b. narcotics.
    c. hallucinogens.
    d. produced only in heavy narcotic users.

ANSWERS

IDENTIFYING THE SUBSTANCE

1. cocaine
2. marijuana
3. heroin
4. barbiturates
5. alcohol
6. caffeine
7. LSD
8. crack cocaine
9. alcohol
10. amphetamine

MATCHING

1. n
2. m
3. i
4. j
5. l
6. b
7. f
8. k
9. h
10. d
11. c
12. g
13. e
14. o
15. a

PUZZLE

A
ADH
ABUSE
SYNANON
MARIJUANA
ACAMPROSATE
TOLERANCE
COCAINE
CRASH
LSD
A

SHORT ANSWER

1.

Medication	Intent
Benzodiazepines	Manage symptoms of withdrawal and delirium tremens.
Acamprosate	Reduce desire for alcohol by acting on the GABA neurotransmitter system.
Citalopram	Reduce desire for alcohol by inhibiting the uptake of serotonin.
Buspirone	Reduce desire for alcohol by inhibiting the uptake of serotonin.
Naltrexone	Reduces pleasurable feelings associated with alcohol use by altering opioid receptors.
Disulfiram	Produces aversive reaction to alcohol by causing a violently unpleasant reaction when mixed with alcohol.

2.

Psychoactive Substance	Subjective effects	Tolerance and dependence	With-drawal	Risks or long-term effects
Alcohol	**Small amounts**: sedative effects **Larger amounts**: disinhibition **Very large amounts**: sleepiness, uncoordination, dysphoria, irritability	Yes	Yes	Brain damage, liver disease, damage to the gastrointestinal system, osteoporosis, cancer, reduced functioning of immune system.
Amphetamines	**Moderate amounts**: euphoria, confidence, talkativeness, energy. **Large amounts**: surge or "rush" of extremely pleasurable sensations.	Yes	Yes	Amphetamine-induced psychosis, also called stimulant psychosis.
Cocaine	**Moderate doses**: Euphoria, sexual excitement, potency, energy, and talkativeness; **Higher doses**: delusions, hallucinations, confusion, suspicion, agitation, and violence.	Yes	Yes	Heart failure and convulsions.
Cannabis (Marijuana)	**Moderate doses**: relaxation and feeling that time is slowed down, heightened sensual enjoyment, hunger, greater awareness of surroundings, possible impairment of short-term memory; **Higher doses**: visual hallucinations and paranoid delusions.	Not clear from available evidence	No	Nasal and respiratory problems, higher risk of cancer and cardiovascular disease, negative effects on reproductive functioning particularly in men; possible loss of motivation; increased risk of accidents.
Hallucinogens	**LSD**: Dizziness, weakness, euphoria, hallucinations; **Psilocybin**: relaxation and euphoria; **PCP**: low doses like depressant; larger doses cause distorted perceptions that can lead to violence..	Information not in text.		**LSD**: Flashbacks and hallucinogen persisting perception disorder. **PCP**: coma, convulsions, brain damage, disorientation so severe that it can lead to accidental death.
Opioids	Intensely pleasurable physical sensations and subjective feelings of euphoria.	Yes	Yes	Highly addictive. Long-term effects: decrease in respiratory efficiency, high blood pressure, and difficulty withdrawing.
Barbiturates	**Low doses**: feeling of calm and sedation, outgoingness, talkativeness, euphoria. **Higher doses**: sleep.	Yes	Yes	Accidental suicide due to respiratory failure. Alcohol potentiates the effect of these drugs, so risk is greater when they are combined with alcohol.
Barbiturate-like substances	Dissociation, loss of inhibitions, greater euphoria during sexual encounters.	Yes	Not discussed in text	Not discussed in text
Anxiolytics	Calm and relaxation.	Yes	Yes	Text discussion includes only withdrawal symptoms, which can be severe.

3. Wernicke and Korsakoff: names of dementias associated with long-term heavy alcohol consumption.
    Cue exposure and relapse prevention: two psychological treatments for alcohol dependence.
    Cocaine and caffeine: stimulants.
    Endorphins and enkephalins: two natural pain-reducing substances in the nervous system.
    Tolerance and withdrawal: two patterns associated with substance dependence.

4. Alcohol is responsible for more than half of the fatal automobile accidents in the U.S.
    Intoxicated pedestrians are four times more likely than nonintoxicated pedestrians to be hit by a car.
    Alcohol increases the risks of accidental drownings, falls, fires, and burns.
    Greater likelihood of serious trauma when an intoxicated person is involved in an accident.
    Increased risk of domestic violence as indicated by the finding that almost two-thirds of husbands who abused their wives were under the influence of alcohol when violent.

5.

Area of investigation	Available evidence
Patterns of inheritance	Higher concordance rate among identical than fraternal twins. Sons of alcoholics are four times more likely to become alcohol dependent than are sons of nonalcoholic parents, and the risk is higher for children of alcoholics regardless of whether they are raised by their biological parents or not.
Biological markers	Subjective reaction to alcohol: Nonalcoholic children of alcoholics show less of a subjective reaction than do children of nonalcoholics. P300 wave: Similar to alcoholics, children of alcoholic fathers show a lowering of the P300 wave after presentation of a stimulus.
Neurotransmitter functioning	Abnormalities have been examined in the GABA, serotonin, and dopamine neurotransmitter systems.
Search for an "alcohol" gene	Attempts have been made to find an "alcohol" gene that influences dopamine receptors but so far have been unsuccessful.

6. In the case of alcohol dependence, alcohol is so much a part of Western society that people may not even realize that excessive consumption is a problem.
    Alcohol dependent individuals tend to deny that they have a problem.
    The individual may be unwilling to reveal the problem to others.
    There is an inherently reinforcing property of psychoactive substance use.
    The painful nature of withdrawal symptoms makes it difficult for the user to achieve abstinence.

7.
a. Alcohol-dependent individuals are faced with the temptation to have a drink and at some point fail to abstain; according to the abstinence violation effect, if the individual's self-efficacy is lowered, a relapse is likely .
b. Decision-making for analyzing situations presenting a high risk of alcohol use.
    Skill training to express and receive feelings, initiate contact with others, and reply to criticism.
    Alternate coping methods for handling high-risk situations.
    Self-efficacy for maintaining abstinence.
c. Alcoholism is an illness or disease.
    A person never completely recovers from alcoholism, no matter how long abstinence has been maintained.
d. Avoid self-blame for lapses from abstinence.
    Develop alternate coping skills for handling situations involving potential alcohol use.
    Receive help through support and contact with others.
    Be motivated to participate in treatment.
e.

Alcoholics Anonymous	Relapse prevention
Control over drinking is seen as due to an outside force.	Control over drinking is seen as due to internal factors.
The client is encouraged to seek help from outside.	The client learns to draw on personal coping resources.

MULTIPLE CHOICE

1.	d	6.	c	11.	d	16.	d
2.	b	7.	d	12.	a	17.	a
3.	a	8.	a	13.	c	18.	b
4.	a	9.	d	14.	d	19.	c
5.	b	10	a	15.	d	20.	a

CHAPTER 15
IMPULSE-CONTROL DISORDERS AND EATING DISORDERS

LEARNING OBJECTIVES

1.0 The Nature of Impulse Control Disorders
    1.1 Identify the essential features common to the impulse control disorders.
2.0 Kleptomania
    2.1 Summarize the characteristics of kleptomania.
    2.2 Indicate the relevant theories and treatments of kleptomania.
3.0 Pathological Gambling
    3.1 Describe the symptoms of pathological gambling.
    3.2 Contrast the theoretical perspectives used to understand and treat pathological gambling.
4.0 Pyromania
    4.1 Indicate the diagnostic features of pyromania.
    4.2 Discuss theories and treatments of pyromania.
5.0 Sexual Impulsivity
    5.1 Outline the characteristic behaviors associated with sexual impulsivity.
    5.2 Indicate the theoretical understanding and treatment of sexual impulsivity.
6.0 Trichotillomania
    6.1 Describe the symptoms used to diagnose trichotillomania.
    6.2 Compare perspectives to understanding and treating the disorder.
7.0 Intermittent Explosive Disorder
    7.1 Summarize the features of intermittent explosive disorder.
    7.2 Describe relevant theories and treatments.
8.0 Eating Disorders
    8.1 Indicate the characteristics of anorexia nervosa.
    8.2 Identify the features of bulimia nervosa.
    8.3 Compare perspectives to understanding and treating eating disorders.
9.0 Impulse Control and Eating Disorders: The Perspectives Revisited
    9.1 Evaluate the evidence linking these disorders to the "affective spectrum."
10.0. Chapter Boxes
    10.1 Indicate the issues involved in the widespread availability of legalized gambling.
    10.2 Discuss the impact of social factors on the development of eating disorders in contemporary society.
    10.3 Evaluate the evidence linking dieting behaviors to the development of eating disorders.

IDENTIFYING TREATMENTS

Write the name of the impulse control disorder or disorders for which the treatment described on the right is used.

1._____	Covert sensitization.		7. _____	Behavioral contracting.
_____			8. _____	Cognitive restructuring.
2._____	Substitute alternative behaviors for the impulsive act.	9. _____	Enhance self-esteem.
_____			10. _____	Aversive conditioning.
3._____	Imaginal desensitization.		_____	
4._____	Self-monitoring.		11. _____	Hypnosis.
5._____	Graphing technique.		12. _____	Relapse prevention.
6._____	Relaxation.			

MATCHING

Put the letter from the right-hand column corresponding to the correct match in the blank next to each item in the left-hand column.

1. ___ Neurotransmitter system thought to play a role in the development of kleptomania, pyromania, intermittent explosive disorder, and eating disorders.
2. ___ A behavioral technique used in the treatment of pyromania.
3. ___ Physical disorder thought to be linked to intermittent explosive disorder.
4. ___ Type of bulimia nervosa in which the individual tries to force out of the body excess food taken in during a binge by vomiting or using laxatives.
5. ___ Term used to identify personality type seen in childhood firestarters characterized by hyperactivity and proneness to destruction and thievery.
6. ___ Hormone that may be present in unusually high levels in individuals with sexual impulsivity.
7. ___ Psychiatrist who established the first U.S. clinic for treatment of pathological gambling.
8. ___ Axis II disorder thought to be linked to eating disorder.
9. ___ A well-known sports figure who was publicly exposed as a pathological gambler.
10. ___ Medication found to be effective in reducing kleptomanic behavior.
11. ___ Type of bulimia nervosa in which the individual tries to compensate for binges by engaging in fasting or excessive exercise.
12. ___ A bet that results in a large amount of money and is influential in propelling an individual to become a pathological gambler.
13. ___ A serial murderer also known as "Son of Sam" who set more than 2000 fires in New York City during the 1970s.
14. ___ Term used to identify a personality type seen in childhood firestarters characterized by mood swings, intense anger, phobias, and tendency toward violence.
15. ___ Psychological disorder thought to be linked to trichotillomania.

a.   testosterone
b.   borderline psychotic
c.   Robert Custer
d.   obsessive-compulsive disorder
e.   big win
f.   Pete Rose
g.   serotonin
h.   nonpurging type
i.   impulsive neurotic
j.   fluoxetine
k.   David Berkowitz
l.   graphing technique
m.   borderline personality disorder
n.   purging type
o.   epilepsy

ANSWERS TO CASE THOUGHT QUESTIONS

Try answering each of the thought questions in boxed clinical vignettes in the chapter. Then read the responses provided here for each case and compare them with yours. If your answers are very different from those we have provided, you should then re-read the relevant sections of the text that pertain to the diagnosis exemplified in the case.

Kleptomania (p. 456)	**Pathological Gambling (p. 460)**
Before shoplifting, Gloria feels tension relieved only by stealing. Further, her stealing is not motivated by a need for the items she steals, as she can afford to pay for them. Finally, Gloria is unable to control her impulse to steal.	After experiencing a "big win" in the form of a $5000 pay-off, Wayne continued to seek the reinforcement of another win. Perhaps he was driven by the fantasy of living a more upscale lifestyle.
Although she has an adequate salary and important job, Gloria is under considerable stress. Earlier in her life she dealt with stress by engaging in shoplifting behavior, and her current involvement in this behavior may be related to an exacerbation of stress in her life.	Wayne does not seem to experience pleasure but feels deeply anxious and troubled by each loss. He is driven by the belief that his losses will very soon be replaced by gain. When he does win, the pleasure he experiences only drives him further into continued betting.

Pyromania (p. 462)	Sexual Impulsivity (p. 464)
People with pyromania become engrossed by the sight of a fire in a way that is starkly different from the ways in which other people would view a fire. In all likelihood, Floyd's ostensible fascination would have raised the suspicions of an astute observer. Floyd was not setting fires for financial gain as is the case with arsonists.	Unlike a person with a paraphilia who is preoccupied with aberrant sexual behavior, there is nothing unusual about Raj's choice of sexual activities. What is unusual is his compulsive need to engage in sexual activity. Raj is unable to control his impulses, shows increasing tension prior to committing the act, and experiences a sense of relief when completing the act.
Trichotillomania (p. 465)	**Intermittent Explosive Disorder (p. 466)**
Janet was an unhappy and isolated child, and now chronically feels depressed and hopeless. For some reason, she has come to engage in hair-pulling behavior which serves as a transient relief to her emotional pain. A dermatologist would notice short broken hairs around the bald spots indicating that the hair had been plucked.	An individual with antisocial personality disorder may act in violent ways, but would not experience any regret after harming others or destroying property. Ed should have a complete medical workup with particular attention to the possibility of neurological disorders such as epilepsy.
Anorexia Nervosa (p. 469)	**Bulimia Nervosa (p. 471)**
Lorraine has stopped eating, has a distorted body image of herself as overweight, has a fear of gaining weight and becoming fat, and has experienced menstrual changes. Correspondence between enrollment in college and the onset of Lorraine's eating disorder suggests that it was difficult for her to separate from home or that she is under pressure from her new peers.	A physician might notice signs of bulimia nervosa such as decaying teeth, sores around the mouth, calluses on the fingers, and swollen salivary glands. Cynthia does not have the symptoms of distorted body image or menstrual disturbances.

WORD SCRAMBLE PUZZLE

This puzzle is like the popular word game in which players form words from tiles that each have a certain value. The following letters are the ones in your "pile" with their assigned values. These letters can be combined in different ways to form the words described in the clues at the left. When you arrange the letters correctly, you will have the point value listed in parentheses. You can use each letter more than once to solve the clues.

Letter	Value	Letter	Value	Letter	Value	Letter	Value
A	1	H	4	N	1	T	1
B	3	I	1	O	1	U	1
C	3	K	5	P	3	V	4
E	1	L	1	R	1	X	8
G	2	M	3	S	1	Y	4

1. A form of impulse control disorder characterized by a persistent and compelling urge to start fires (16 points).
2. An impulse control disorder involving the persistent urge to steal (19 points).
3. In intermittent _____ disorder, the individual experiences uncontrollable violent bursts of anger (21 points).
4. In the eating disorder _____ nervosa, the individual has a view of herself as overweight even though she may be near starvation (15 points).

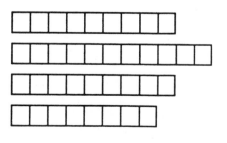

5. The behavior engaged in by individuals with eating disorders when they attempt to rid themselves of food they have already eaten (11 points).

☐☐☐☐☐☐☐

6. In _____ nervosa, the individual may maintain a normal weight though she yields to uncontrollable urges to overeat and then rid herself of what she has eaten (11 points).

☐☐☐☐☐☐☐

7. An uncontrollable urge to act is called an _____ (11 points).

☐☐☐☐☐☐☐

8. An impulse control disorder involving the uncontrollable and compulsive urge to pull out one's hair (23 points).

☐☐☐☐☐☐☐☐☐☐☐☐☐☐☐

SHORT ANSWER

1. What are three essential features of the behavior of people with an impulse-control disorder?

_____   _____

_____

2. For each of the following disorders, describe a somatic treatment found to be helpful in reducing symptoms and the proposed mechanism of action of this treatment:

Disorder	Somatic treatment	Mechanism of action
Kleptomania		
Sexual impulsivity		
Trichotillomania		
Intermittent explosive disorder		
Eating disorders		

3. What are the two key differences between anorexia nervosa and bulimia nervosa?

_____

_____

4. Describe the role of faulty cognitions in the development of pathological gambling and eating disorders:

Disorder	Role of faulty cognitions
Pathological gambling	
Eating disorders	

5. What three lines of evidence regarding the relationship between mood disorders and impulse control disorders support the contention that these disorders are on the same "affective spectrum?"

_____

_____

_____

6. Summarize the main features of each of the following stages involved in the development of pathological gambling:

Stage	Main features
Recreational gambling	

Stage	Main features
Early winning stage	
The big win	
Chasing	
Establishment of pathological gambling cycle	

7. Describe the hypothesized role of family relationships in the development or maintenance of the following disorders:

Disorder	Role of family relationships
Pathological gambling	
Sexual impulsivity	
Trichotillomania	
Eating disorders	

MULTIPLE CHOICE

1. During the course of committing an impulsive act, people with impulse control disorders:
   a. usually feel tension and anxiety immediately after engaging in the impulsive act.
   b. may experience arousal before engaging in the impulsive act that they liken to sexual excitement.
   c. feel intensely conflicted at the moment of choosing to engage in the impulsive act.
   d. often experience feelings of regret and remorse immediately before engaging in the impulsive act.

2. Which of the following statements is true regarding people with kleptomania?
   a. They are driven by a desire to accumulate expensive possessions.
   b. They limit their stealing to situations in which they are taking items from people whom they know personally.
   c. They are driven by the desire to steal, not the desire to have.
   d. They rarely suffer from psychological disorders other than the problem of kleptomania.

3. Researchers investigating the role of biological factors in pathological gambling have found that these individuals:
   a. show more norepinephrine activity than non-gamblers.
   b. have thyroid abnormalities.
   c. have lower levels of dopamine than non-gamblers.
   d. show evidence of specific biological markers.

4. A treatment of pathological gambling involving clients imagining scenes in which they feel tempted to gamble, and relaxing as they imagine each successive behavior involved in the scene:
   a. covert sensitization.
   b. flooding.
   c. in vivo desensitization.
   d. imaginal desensitization.

5. Type of bulimia nervosa in which one rids the body of food with vomiting, laxatives, or diuretics:
   a. anorexic
   b. purging
   c. depressive
   d. nonpurging

6. According to government estimates, the highest rates for legalized gambling occur in states in which:
   a. casinos are built in expensive resort areas.
   b. gambling has been legalized for many years.
   c. there are lotteries but not casinos.
   d. new casinos and lotteries were developed.

7. Prior to engaging in a seemingly uncontrollable act, people with intermittent explosive disorder experience a phenomenon similar to that experienced by people with:
   a. epilepsy.
   b. high blood pressure.
   c. cardiovascular disease.
   d. migraine headache disorder.

8. Research on the relationship between dieting and eating disorders indicates that:
   a. Dieters are at lower risk for developing eating disorders.
   b. There is no relationship between dieting and eating disorders.
   c. Dieters are at greater risk for developing eating disorders.
   d. Exercisers but not dieters are likely to develop eating disorders.

9. Proponents of which theoretical model propose that people with bulimia incorporate society's attitudes toward thinness and translate them into extreme restraints and rigid rules about food?
   a. societal
   b. psychodynamic
   c. family systems
   d. cognitive-behavioral

10. Extreme cases of sexual impulsivity are sometimes treated biologically with
    a. antiandrogenic medication.
    b. testosterone.
    c. ECT.
    d. neuroleptics.

11. According to Custer's views regarding the development of pathological gambling, the transition to becoming a pathological gambler becomes evident when the gambler:
    a. starts to gain an identity as a winner.
    b. starts to develop fears of becoming a loser.
    c. begins to experience family problems.
    d. seeks professional help for the gambling problem.

12. The Goldfarb Fear of Fat Scale would be used in the diagnosis of :
    a. bulimia nervosa.
    b. anorexia nervosa.
    c. eating disorders involving possible medical complications.
    d. any eating disorder.

13. Which behavioral technique involves having the individual with kleptomania imagine disgusting images such as vomit when the compulsion to steal is beginning?
    a. free association
    b. flooding
    c. covert sensitization
    d. in vivo desensitization

14. Which of the following techniques involves having the client with pyromania construct a chart that corresponds to the individual's behaviors, feelings, and experiences associated with firesetting?
    a. the graphing technique
    b. the thought stopping technique
    c. aversive conditioning
    d. in vivo desensitization

15. According to the family systems perspective, adults with sexual impulsivity are more likely to grow up in families with:
    a. restrictive attitudes regarding sex.
    b. permissive attitudes regarding sex.
    c. liberal opinions regarding sex.
    d. open attitudes about sex.

16. Trichotillomania is an impulse control disorder involving the persistent urge to:
    a. pull one's hair.
    b. bite one's nails.
    c. binge, then purge.
    d. engage in sexual intercourse.

17. While stopped in his car at a stop light, Tim occasionally experiences an aura, followed by an intense urge to get out of the car and pummel the person in the car ahead of him for no apparent reason. He has been arrested several times for acting on this urge. What impulse control disorder might Tim suffer from?
    a. antisocial personality disorder
    b. oppositional defiant disorder
    c. intermittent explosive disorder
    d. passive aggressive personality disorder

18. Which of the following is considered to be the core feature of anorexia nervosa?
    a. frequent binging
    b. normal body weight
    c. consumption of nonnutritive substances
    d. body image disturbance

19. Among these countries, the highest rates for anorexia nervosa are found in:
    a. China.
    b. France.
    c. India.
    d. the U.S.

20. In the textbook case, which of the following facts might have led Dr. Tobin to conclude that Neil Gorman's gambling behavior was beyond the boundaries of social gambling?
    a. The fact that he was seeking a big win.
    b. The fact that he started drinking while he was gambling.
    c. The fact that his wife approved of his gambling.
    d. The fact that he promised his wife that he would stop, but did not.

ANSWERS

IDENTIFYING TREATMENTS

1. Kleptomania
   Sexual impulsivity
2. Trichotillomania
   Sexual impulsivity
3. Pathological gambling
4. Eating disorders
5. Pyromania
6. Trichotillomania

7. Sexual impulsivity
8. Eating disorders
9. Sexual impulsivity
   Eating disorders
10. Trichotillomania
    Pathological gambling
11. Trichotillomania
12. Eating disorders

MATCHING

1.	g	6.	a	11.	h
2.	l	7.	c	12.	e
3.	o	8.	m	13.	k
4.	n	9.	f	14.	b
5.	i	10.	j	15.	d

WORD SCRAMBLE

1. PYROMANIA
2. KLEPTOMANIA
3. EXPLOSIVE
4. ANOREXIA
5. PURGING
6. BULIMIA
7. IMPULSE
8. TRICHOTILLOMANIA

SHORT ANSWER

1.   They are unable to stop from acting on impulses that are harmful to self or others.
   Before they act on their impulse, they feel pressured to act.
   Upon acting on their impulse, they feel a sense of pleasure or gratification similar to sexual release.

2.

Disorder	Somatic treatment	Mechanism of action
Kleptomania	Fluoxetine (Prozac)	Increases availability of serotonin
Sexual impulsivity	Antiandrogenic medication	Reduces level of testosterone
Trichotillomania	Lithium Clomipramine	Not described in text Antidepressant that reduces obsessional symptoms
Intermittent explosive disorder	Benzodiazepines Lithium Beta blockers	Used to reduce explosive behavior in people with certain personality disorders. Both reduce emotional reactivity by lowering norepinephrine functioning

Disorder	Somatic treatment	Mechanism of action
Eating disorders	Fluoxetine	Increases availability of serotonin
	Antidepressants	Reduce depressive symptoms and also reduce eating disorder behaviors specifically
	MAO inhibitors	No longer used because of undesirable side effects.

3.   **Body image**: People with anorexia nervosa see themselves as overweight, no matter how emaciated they may be; people with bulimia nervosa have normal body image.

    Amount of weight loss: People with anorexia nervosa are significantly below the norm for weight; people with bulimia are of normal or above average weight.

4.

Disorder	Role of faulty cognitions
Pathological gambling	Pathological gamblers hold the faulty beliefs that they are in control the probabilities that affect the outcome of their bets; this leads them to develop grandiose ideas that lead them to become convinced of their ultimate success
Eating disorders	The individual's incorporation of society's beliefs about thinness leads the individual to adopt a set of rules and restrictions regarding food; in the case of bulimia nervosa, these rules break down when the individual becomes hungry, and a binge pattern is set in motion

5.

a. Several impulse control disorders have been found to co-occur with mood disorders, including kleptomania, pathological gambling, and eating disorders. Trichotillomania is thought to be linked to obsessive-compulsive disorder, another disorder that would fall on a proposed affective spectrum.

b. Altered functioning of serotonin and norepinephrine neurotransmitters, systems that are thought to play a role in mood disorders, have been observed in people with impulse control disorders, including kleptomania, pathological gambling, pyromania, and eating disorders.

c. Treatments used for mood disorders have been successfully applied to the impulse control disorders of kleptomania, trichotillomania, intermittent explosive disorder, and eating disorders.

6.

Stage	Main features
Recreational gambling	The person's behavior is indistinguishable from that of a gambler who enjoys gambling as a social activity.
Early winning stage	The individual begins to win, and starts to gain gambling skills. Development of identity as a "winner" occurs, and through continued wins, that identity becomes reinforced.
The big win	A gain of a large amount of money in one bet is so highly reinforcing that the individual becomes possessed with the need to reexperience it. The gambler is convinced of the possession of unique luck and skill, and starts to make riskier bets.

Stage	Main features
Chasing	After losses inevitably start to occur, the individual begins to bet more and more to recoup earlier losses. As desperation mounts, the individual is launched into an intensive and all-consuming enterprise. Poor judgment combined with desperation lead to larger and larger losses.
Establishment of pathological gambling cycle	In continued search for another big win, the individual has periodic wins that maintain his or her unreasonable optimism. In time, however, the individual's resources become depleted and the person may consider drastic action such as suicide, running away, or a life of crime to support the behavior.

7.

Disorder	Role of family relationships
Pathological gambling	Spouses and children of pathological gamblers are affected by the disorder. Spouses report detrimental changes in emotional functioning, dysfunctional coping behaviors, emotional, verbal, or physical abuse, and feelings of suicidality. Children experience significant behavioral and adjustment problems in school and at home, and involvement in drug or alcohol abuse, crime, or gambling-related activities. Families also suffer financially due to the heavy betting expenses.
Sexual impulsivity	The disorder is thought to result from either unduly restrictive attitudes toward sex in a child's family or as a result of childhood neglect and abuse. The disorder may result in or be maintained in adulthood by dysfunctional communication patterns in the sexual domain between sexual partners.
Trichotillomania	Described in terms of psychodynamic theory, disturbed parent-child relationships are thought to create feelings of neglect, abandonment, or emotional burdening in a child who attempts to gain attention or gratification through hair-pulling.
Eating disorders	Family systems theorists propose that a girl may develop anorexia nervosa in an effort to assert her independence from the family, perhaps in situations where the girl feels that her parents are standing in the way of becoming autonomous. Other contributing factors may be a family that is chaotic, incapable of resolving conflict, unaffectionate, and lacking in empathy.

MULTIPLE CHOICE

1. b	6. b	11. a	16. a
2. c	7. a	12. b	17. c
3. a	8. c	13. c	18. d
4. d	9. d	14. a	19. d
5. b	10 a	15. a	20. d